Practical
BEDDING
PLANTS

Ian Murray

The Crowood Press

First published in 1994 by
The Crowood Press Ltd
Ramsbury, Marlborough
Wiltshire SN8 2HR

British Library Cataloguing-in-Publication Data

A catalogue record for this book is available from the British
Library.

ISBN 1 85223 780 5

Dedication
To my wife, Kathy

Picture Credits
Line-drawings by Claire Upsdale-Jones
All photographs by Ian Murray

Typeset in Optima by Chippendale Type Ltd,
Otley, West Yorkshire
Printed and bound by Paramount Printing Group, Hong Kong

CONTENTS

INTRODUCTION

Technical terms and jargon can cause problems for anyone exploring a new subject, and gardening is no exception; indeed, the definition and classification of plants causes considerable confusion. This is exacerbated when plants are defined rather flexibly, and even the experts are inconsistent in their use of the various terms. Bedding plants especially suffer in this respect: for example, roses are invariably grown in beds and yet they are excluded from the category, while geraniums, which are commonly used as pot plants, are classified as mainstream bedding plants. It is hoped that this book will help to demystify the subject by reflecting the philosophy of ordinary gardeners who are concerned with the plants themselves and not with their classifications. The way in which plants are used should determine their category. This may produce anomalies, but this is unimportant to the business of cultivation.

The essence of bedding is its temporary nature, allowing the creation of a beautiful scene which can be repeated or changed each year, according to personal choice. There are those in gardening circles who deride short-term planting, an attitude which is perhaps rooted in a dislike of the Victorian schemes. And while it is true that geometric layouts and orderliness are the tradition of bedding arrangements, the plants themselves are highly versatile and are easily translated into the current vogue for informal landscape. Whatever the arguments, the question is really one of fashion, whose movement is frequently circular and not necessarily dictated by aesthetic taste.

The garden festivals were famous for their bedding displays. Here at Gateshead, in 1990, tulips are underplanted with pansies.

Do what you will with your garden, and always remember that your satisfaction and enjoyment are the most important achievements.

1 • BUYING PLANTS

Until quite recently, the only bedding plants that could be bought were mature and ready to plant, but nowadays it is possible to buy seedlings and young plants at various stages of growth.

Seedlings

Most of the mail-order seed companies offer seedlings of various plants but the range is very limited and may not exceed ten or a dozen different kinds. These seedlings are grown to order under contract and therefore each company has a deadline after which they will not accept orders. Garden centres are increasing their range and quantity of seedlings, which are cheaper than those from seed companies. All seedlings are available at the stage when they will need pricking out quite soon after purchase. It is important that they are grown on in suitable conditions (*see* page 15).

Plugs

Plugs are small plants that have been grown in trays with individual cells. This system enables the roots to be kept separate and, consequently, the plants to be very easily transplanted. They are larger than seedlings but have further growth to make before they can be planted out. They are most often put into larger cellular trays or into small pots until they are ready for planting out. Plugs are available at various stages of growth from commercial growers.

Seed companies also sell plugs but they are rare in garden centres because the small rooting area means rapid depletion of nutrients and their shelf life is short. This situation will not persist because professional growers are researching new fertilizers that will continue to feed the plants over a longer term, so plugs are destined for much greater popularity with amateur gardeners.

Seedlings in peat pots – Jiffy 7s – can be planted together with the pot when the plant is sufficiently mature.

They are more expensive than seedlings but they are closer to maturity and represent a saving in time and the cost of protection before planting out.

Young Plants

These, too, can be purchased by mail order and from garden centres, although it is usually only expensive bedding subjects that are available. They are often grown in small 'pots' made from compressed peat so they can be planted directly. Cost is a deterrent to purchase but since they are almost mature they are most convenient for planting in tubs and hanging baskets.

Ready-to-Plant

This category represents the major portion of the bedding plant market although there are signs of some change in the situation. Obviously, such plants have been grown

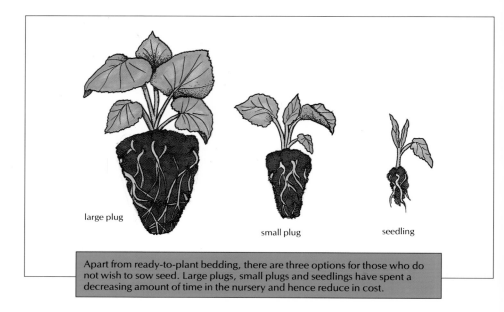

large plug

small plug

seedling

Apart from ready-to-plant bedding, there are three options for those who do not wish to sow seed. Large plugs, small plugs and seedlings have spent a decreasing amount of time in the nursery and hence reduce in cost.

commercially for many weeks and their price reflects the cost of long-term maintenance. However, there is often a huge variation at the point of sale and in some cases, mature bedding is cheaper than large plugs and young plants. This anomaly is entirely due to the growing system and hence the quality of the product.

Traditionally, growers prick out their seedlings into open trays or wooden boxes. By the time the plants near complete development, the containers have become massed with intermingled roots. The full-sized box holds forty or fifty plants depending on variety and some bedding is still sold like this. However, wooden boxes have largely been replaced by thin plastic trays. This is the least expensive form of bedding but since the plants are frequently overcrowded they will not have achieved their optimum growth or quality. Apart from this deficiency, there are problems when planting because of the virtually inseparable roots. The most effective method is to use a large knife to cut the roots, leaving the plants with roughly equal amounts. The same difficulty arises with the strip method of growing: here, the plants are raised in strips of plastic or polystyrene containers which can be separated from each other, but the separation of the plants is never easy.

It is also possible to buy plants that have been raised individually in trays of connected pots (known as packs). Not surprisingly, such plants occupy more space in the grower's greenhouse and are consequently more expensive to raise and there is the added cost of the more elaborate container. The advantages are those of high quality and speedy, uncomplicated planting, which many gardeners believe is ample compensation for the greater unit cost.

Assessing Quality

Some assessment must be made of how

Cellular trays allow plants to grow with minimal competition and permit easy removal – with rootball intact – for planting.

well the plants have been cared for by the retailer. Whereas garden centres have the staff and facilities to maintain high standards, most garden shops are without greenhouse space. This means that many tender plants are exposed to forecourt conditions when the weather is at its most fickle and the damaging consequences may not be apparent until days later.

Sometimes the trays of bedding plants are not properly labelled and for the conscientious gardener, this can be most frustrating. Simply to indicate that the plants are marigolds is not sufficient. There are dozens of marigold varieties currently available. Are they yellow, gold, red or mixed? Six or twenty-six inches tall? Single or double flowers? It is a simple and low cost matter to identify them with the essential details and include some cultivation hints as well. Happily, this is a diminishing irritation largely because of the urging of the Bedding Plant Association and the example set by the principal growers.

A more serious complaint is that plants are often offered for sale too early in the season. When the public sees the retail displays there is a natural assumption that it is the appropriate time to buy and to plant; this is far from true and much disappointment arises from premature planting when the late spring weather reveals the nastier side of its character. It is a market-driven problem as the earliest plants fetch the highest prices and growers are naturally reluctant to withhold their bedding from eager retailers. The gardening public could change the whole situation by refusing to buy but they are lured by the attractive plants and impatient for the new season to begin. Perhaps it is advisable to purchase good-quality plants when they are seen but keep them protected until the weather indicators are favourable.

2 • SOWING SEED

The easiest way to obtain a bedding plant display is to visit the local garden centre and buy plants that are ready for planting. However, while the cost of buying a few plants may be inconsequential, it can be extremely expensive if you require large numbers. Another drawback is that commercially grown plants are usually available in only a few bedding varieties, and colour choice is especially limited because mixed colours are popularly sold and it is often difficult to buy plants in particular shades.

If you are prepared to put in the extra effort required, it is worth buying seed instead. It affords the opportunity of growing species that are virtually unknown to the general public and also allows the choice of varieties that will fit the desired colour scheme. Obviously, the cost of a packet of seed compares very favourably with expenditure on mature plants but the economics of seed-raised subjects is more complicated. Many of our favourite flowers come from kind climates and need an

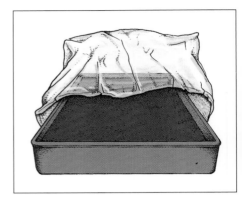

If you do not have a propagator, place the seed tray in a plastic bag. This will protect germination and provide the humid atmosphere that is essential for seed sown on the surface of the compost.

appropriate temperature regime to develop satisfactorily. A heated environment is essential and the consequent cost must be considered in the price equation, although raising seeds in the home, especially in the early stages, can be most effective.

The ideal conditions can be provided by a heated propagator, or a greenhouse or conservatory, which is maintained at a suitable level of warmth. Nevertheless, it is entirely possible to achieve good results by using an airing cupboard for germinating seed and allowing the young plants to grow on the kitchen or living room windowsill. Some of the more difficult plants would not thrive with this domestic improvisation but those that germinate and grow quickly can be very successful.

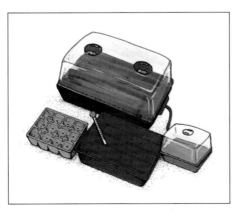

Many gardeners manage very well with improvised seed-raising equipment but the advantages of specialized items are immeasurable. A heated or unheated propagator simplifies the task, and a thermometer and a cellular tray are most desirable.

Buying Seed

Garden centres and most garden retailers sell packet seed. The range of varieties offered will satisfy most gardeners, although a much larger choice is offered in the catalogues. Some of the seed companies operate a mail order only system and their seed is not sold by retail outlets.

Whether buying locally or directly from seed companies, it is advisable to collect some catalogues because many of them are well illustrated and contain a great deal of useful reference material for gardeners. All the companies offer some varieties that are exclusive to them and new introductions are a tempting prospect for gardeners who want something innovative and perhaps different from commonly grown subjects. It may be helpful to do some price comparisons between various companies but generally this exercise is not entirely revealing.

Unlike vegetable seeds, flower seeds are not subject to any regulations that require a guarantee of germination rate and although most seed companies do test batches of seed for their own purpose, the information is not passed on to the public. In recent years, most companies have begun to reveal how many seeds there are in the packet but the purchaser has no way of knowing what percentage is likely to germinate. A couple of the companies do indicate the number of plants likely to result from each packet and one of the more progressive companies gives the general reassurance that a germination percentage of 70 should be expected.

The viability of seed is affected by its age and storage conditions and almost all companies use vacuum-sealed foil or cellophane containers within the outer packet. This excludes air and moisture and is an excellent preservative measure but only the company knows the age of the seed. It seems likely, judging from independent tests, that some retail seed companies do sell older seed of some varieties. The only way of gaining this information is to read the reports made by the major consumer organizations, such as *Gardening Which?* in the United Kingdom who make an annual judgement based on practical tests.

Perhaps only the most conscientious consumers will go to these lengths in search of dependable quality but it is important that all growers insist on value for money and the reduction of potential disappointment. If the instructions on the seed packet are followed and the results are poor then a complaint should be made to the company. Invariably, this will result in reimbursement or a replacement packet. The major users of bedding plant seed – commercial growers and the parks – use the wholesale seed companies which are largely unknown to the domestic gardener. The highest quality seed is sold and represents the best possible value for money. However, even the smallest packets that they sell are much too large

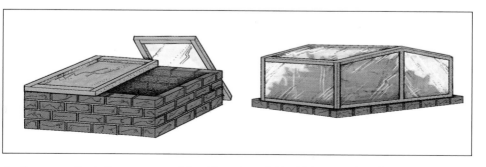

For the more enthusiastic grower, a traditional frame is available. (Right) A modern aluminium cold frame.

for the ordinary gardener, although there is no reason why a group of friends or neighbours should not make a pooled order.

Sowing the Seed

Growing Conditions

Some equipment is necessary to achieve consistent success with raising plants from seed and a protected environment is essential for growing the seedlings to maturity. It

A special clip converts two panes of glass into a cloche.

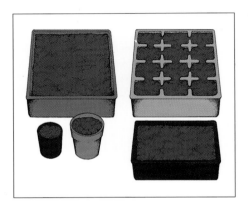

A variety of containers for sowing and pricking out seedlings.

is possible to use commonplace substitutes such as an ordinary seed-tray enclosed in a plastic bag placed inside the airing cupboard which is unquestionably the most reliably warm situation in the home. Clearly it is not ideal for those seeds that require light for optimum germination, but it will achieve reasonable results with care. An important proviso is that the seed-tray must be examined daily and, as soon as growth is detected, the seedlings must be removed from the dark and accommodated on a bright and warm windowsill.

The superior alternative to this is an electrically heated propagator, preferably with thermostatic control, which will provide a moist, warm atmosphere and maintain a steady temperature. This facility involves capital outlay but it is normally trouble free, lasts for many years and, apart from cleaning, there is no maintenance. Any enthusiastic gardener can regard a propagator as a cost-effective purchase because it is also useful for rooting cuttings and perfect for overwintering tender subjects.

The Sowing Process

Normal potting compost is suitable for sowing, and any receptacle that has holes in the base to drain superfluous water can be used. Strict cleanliness is desirable if troubles are to be avoided because numerous pathogens will take advantage of warmth and humidity and young plants are susceptible to various disorders. Clean, new compost together with washed and disinfected containers are prerequisites to avoiding potential problems.

Large seeds are easily dispensed, either sprinkled from the packet or placed individually by finger and thumb with the aim of providing sufficient space for the seedlings to develop without overcrowding. The depth of planting will be indicated on the

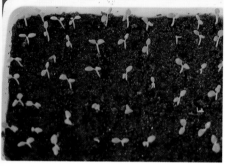

Geranium seed is quite large and should be sown thinly to allow sufficient space for early growth.

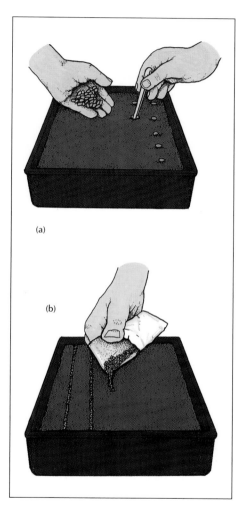

seed packet together with the other important information but generally, larger seed should be covered by about 6mm (¼in) of compost.

Small seed presents the principal difficulty for amateurs and some is unbelievably tiny – begonias have approximately 70,000 seeds per gram! It is also more valuable by weight than gold, and so considerable care is needed: a badly timed sneeze will be very expensive. Often, the smallest seed is difficult to see and precautions should be taken to eliminate waste and to distribute the minute specks as thinly as possible over the compost. Tap the packet vigorously so that the seed drops to the bottom and open the top over the compost so that wayward seeds do not fall to the floor. It is helpful to

Large seed (a) can be conveniently spaced out by hand or with tweezers. Fine seed (b) should be gently tapped from the packet and sown thinly.

conduct proceedings in good light so that subsequent distribution can be seen easily and can be as even as is practicable. This ensures that each seed can germinate without undue competition and that later

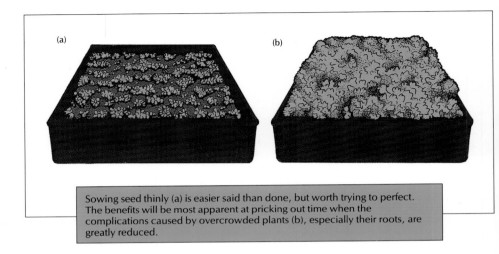

Sowing seed thinly (a) is easier said than done, but worth trying to perfect. The benefits will be most apparent at pricking out time when the complications caused by overcrowded plants (b), especially their roots, are greatly reduced.

growth does not lead to the roots becoming hopelessly entwined, which will impede the later stage of pricking out. The final point to make about extremely small seed is

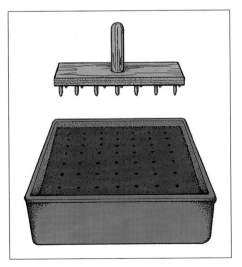

A Dibalot firms the compost and makes holes at regular intervals which is ideal for large seeds or pricking out.

that it should be sown on the surface of the compost and not covered. Watering is best effected with a hand spray so that the seed is not buried. It is vital that the uppermost compost does not dry out during germination otherwise losses will occur and thus a moist atmosphere is essential during the propagating period.

Germination

The way in which an apparently inert capsule is transformed into dynamic vegetation is one of the wonders of life, fraught with apparent complications but easily accomplished by gardeners. The fundamental requirements of moisture, air and optimum temperature enable growth to proceed without human intervention but there are some obstacles to success. Evolution has determined that different seeds require different temperatures for different periods and the coating of some seed contains inhibitors to prevent germination occurring inappropriately. Fortunately, most bedding seed is simply stirred into growth although some species need a spell of low temperatures or

Young geranium seedlings benefit from growing in cellular trays.

even frost before the embryonic plant is activated. Some seed is 'primed' before it is sold, a process that removes the inhibitors and allows prompt germination.

Lining the greenhouse with bubble plastic conserves heat and reduces cold spots near the glass.

Once the seedlings have emerged, they can be removed from the propagating conditions but they must be kept away from cold draughts and direct sunshine. After a week or so of acclimatization, they can be increasingly exposed to cooler air and brighter light.

Pricking Out

The task of pricking out does not attract many enthusiasts because it requires concentration and some manipulative skills together with a patient approach to avoid damaging seedlings. If the seedlings are large enough to be handled they should be gently separated and if a pencil or small stick is used to lever the roots out of the compost, the process is greatly eased. The small plants must be held only by the leaves and no attempt should be made to pull them without ensuring that the roots are not

Seedlings should always be pricked out by holding a leaf and using a small stick to ease the roots gently out of the soil. Watering through a fine rose or with a hand sprayer will settle the plants in position.

secured in the compost. When the seedling is safely extracted, a hole can be made in the receiving compost which will

Cellular trays allow plants to grow without competition.

accommodate the roots without cramping. The compost is then pushed back over the roots and gently firmed around the stem. Only light pressure should be used because the plant will be settled in its new position by watering with a fine rose when the tray is fully planted.

In some cases, especially if pricking out has been delayed, the roots of seedlings may have tangled with each other, but they can be teased apart with care. Ideally, pricking out should be done when the plants can be easily held but before the roots have spread widely. The best containers for growing the seedlings on are those with individual compartments so that subsequent growth is not impeded by competition and planting out at a later stage presents no difficulties. Large seedlings, like geraniums, can be pricked out directly into small pots.

Larger seedlings like geraniums can be pricked out into small pots but this is not advisable for small seedlings or those that grow slowly.

Growing On

Maximum light soon becomes the primary consideration to encourage sturdy, healthy growth. Although the temperature regime is less critical at this stage, tender plants need continued protection. Some species will suffer when the air temperature drops below 13°C (55°F), and cultivators who grow on seeds on the windowsill should be aware that close proximity to the glass on cold nights can chill the plants severely. In heated conservatories and greenhouses, it is normally a simple matter to position plants where the warmth is adequate. It is by no means necessary to heat the whole structure to the preferred minimum temperature: plastic sheeting makes a convenient and

temporary partition or especially susceptible plants can be positioned close to the source of heat until the weather becomes warmer.

After a week or so of coddling, the intention should be progressively to accustom the plants to a cooler regime and eventually to 'harden them off' gradually to the harsh reality of the outside world. It must be remembered that frost is a killer and the majority of bedding plants would at least be damaged by exposure to it; they should be protected until sub-zero temperatures are no longer likely.

Sowing Outdoors

The traditional method of raising those plants that fall into the category of hardy annuals is to sow them directly into the garden soil, but even with these rugged individuals there are inherent problems. Small seed begets small seedlings, which are easily damaged by heavy rainfall or wandering cats and dogs, not to mention birds. Large seed produces larger seedlings but even the larger plants are prone to physical damage in their early stages

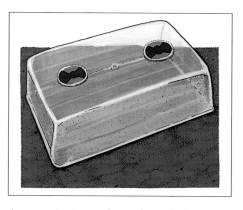

A propagator top can be used as a cloche to protect outdoor sowings.

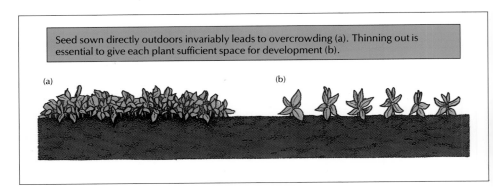

Seed sown directly outdoors invariably leads to overcrowding (a). Thinning out is essential to give each plant sufficient space for development (b).

(a)

(b)

although there are less obvious difficulties for all outdoor sowing.

Weed seeds are present in all garden soil and distinguishing the plant seedlings from those of weeds is a severe test, even for experienced gardeners. Often when the weeds have reached the stage when they can more easily be recognized, they have reached the size at which their removal will cause disruption in the flower bed. The flower seedlings will not have grown so quickly and as the weeds are pulled out, so too is the future flower display.

For these reasons, even hardy annuals are better sown in trays, either indoors or outdoors. The seedlings can be transplanted when they have sufficient stature to resist the vagaries of life in the open garden. If it is decided to sow directly into beds, the whole area should be rigorously weeded and lightly hoed and levelled, ensuring that the surface is made up of fine particles of soil. The seed should be sown thinly but it will still be necessary to thin out overcrowded seedlings and to ensure that those remaining are separated by sufficient space to allow proper development.

To Sow or Not to Sow

Some people will be deterred from raising their own plants because of the implicit complications or the expenditure on equipment, or simply because they are mystified by what they consider to be a very complicated process. Actually, the technique is quickly learned and, provided that the packet instructions are followed, success becomes a high probability.

In almost every instance, sowing seed rather than buying plants offers a reasonable financial saving and there is a definite sense of achievement in completing the task from packet to glorious display. The secret, if there is one, is properly to identify those subjects that present real cultivation difficulties and to concentrate instead on those that germinate readily and grow robustly. The more awkward bedding plants can always be purchased, at various stages of growth, until such time as the expertise has been gained or the enthusiasm can no longer be denied.

In a book of this size, there is insufficient space to make a comprehensive list of plants that can be used for bedding, although Chapters 7 to 9 list the most popular ones, and more are described in *Bedding Plants: Step by Step to Growing Success*, published by Crowood. However, seed catalogues are excellent in this respect and include literally hundreds of different

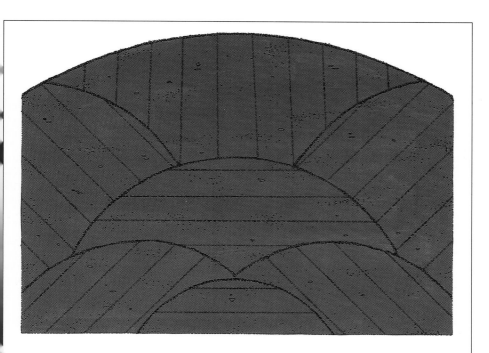

Direct sowing is best done in 'drifts': mark out rounded areas, with seed drills at angles to each other. This helps to give a natural look to direct sown flowers.

Circular and semi-circular areas are simply achieved with a marking stick, string and a stake.

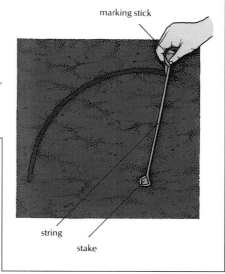

marking stick

string

stake

varieties. Some catalogues are lavishly illustrated and one or two include miscellaneous gardening items that are available by mail order, but all the catalogues endeavour each year to offer some seed that is exclusive to them, and all contain useful reference material and practical tips for successful sowing.

Notes to the seed sowing tables

The temperature range in the tables is that which will give optimum germination results but most seed will germinate outside the range given although the results will usually be slower and more erratic. The temperatures listed should be that of the compost in which the seed is sown.

Pre-soaking in warm water is beneficial for some hard-coated seeds. Those which show signs of swelling should be sown; those which do not can be chipped with a file. The purpose is to damage the hard seed coat so that moisture can penetrate.

Most seed will germinate satisfactorily in the light or the dark but where the table remarks recommend surface sowing or only a light covering of compost, this indicates that germination will be much better in a light position – but not in direct sunshine.

High humidity, when it is required, can be easily achieved by placing the seed par or pot in a plastic bag.

The time taken for seedlings to emerge can be variable, especially if the preferred temperature range is not maintained.

The recommended sowing dates are intended as a guide for an 'average' year in which the late frosts finish by the end of May.

All the hardy annuals (**HA**) can be sown outdoors, in the ground or in containers, from early spring onwards; the hardy perennials (**HP**) can be sown outdoors in the summer.

Note: the months listed in the sowing tables refer to the Northern hemisphere. Gardeners in the Southern hemisphere should read June for January, July for February and so on.

SOWING TABLES

NAME	TYPE	TEMPERATURES °F	(°C)	TIME WEEKS	GERMINATION SOWING DATE	REMARKS
Abutilon	**HHP**	65–70	(18–21)	3-4	Feb/Mar	
Ageratum	**HHA**	65–70	(18–21)	1½–2	Mar/Apr	
Althaea	**HA**	55–60	(13–16)	1½–2½	Feb	
Alyssum	**HA**	55–65	(13–18)	1½–2	Mar	Lightly cover seed
Alyssum saxatile	**HP**	55–65	(13–18)	2–3	Jun	Do not cover seed
Amaranthus	**HHA**	70–75	(21–24)	2–4	Feb	
Anchusa	**HA**	65–75	(18–24)	2–3	Mar	
Antirrhinum	**HHA**	65–75	(18–24)	2–3	Feb	Lightly cover seed
Arabis	**HP**	60–70	(16–21)	2–4	Jun	Barely cover seed
Arctotis	**HHA**	60–70	(16–21)	3–4	Mar	Care with watering
Asarina	**HHA**	65–70	(18–21)	2–3	Feb	Prick out into pots
Aster	**HHA**	65–70	(18–21)	1½–2	Mar/Apr	
Atriplex	**HHA**	65–75	(18–24)	2–3	Apr	
Aubretia	**HP**	60–70	(16–21)	2–4	Jun	Do not cover seed
Auricula	**HP**	60–70	(16–21)	3–5	Jun	Must be kept moist
Begonia (tuberous)	**HHP**	65–70	(18–21)	2–3	Dec/Mar	Supplementary light needed if sown before March. Surface sow and maintain maximum humidity
Begonia semperflorens	**HHA**	65–75	(18–24)	2–3	Jan/Feb	Surface sow and maintain maximum humidity

SOWING TABLES

NAME	TYPE	TEMPERATURES °F	(°C)	TIME WEEKS	GERMINATION SOWING DATE	REMARKS
Bellis	HB	55–65	(13–18)	2–3	May/Jun	
Brachycome	HHA	65–80	(18–27)	2–4	Mar	Barely cover seed
Brassica	HA	50–60	(10–16)	1½–3	Mar/Apr	
Calceolaria	HHA	60–70	(16–21)	2–3	Feb	
Calendula	HA	55–65	(13–18)	1½–3	Apr	
Campsis	HHA	70–75	(21–24)	4–12	Dec/Jan	Do not cover seed
Candytuft	HP	65–75	(18–24)	1½–4	May/Jun	Often erratic germination
Canna	HHP	70–80	(21–27)	3–10	Jan/Feb	Soak seed for 24 hours. Often erratic germination
Cardiospermum	HHA	70–80	(21–27)	3–5	Jan	
Carnation	HP	60–70	(16–21)	1½–2½	Feb	
Celosia	HHA	65–80	(18–27)	1½–3	Mar/Apr	Ensure compost is moist
Centaurea	HA	60–75	(16–24)	1–2½	Mar	
Cerastium	HP	55–70	(13–21)	1½–3	Mar/Apr	
Chrysanthemum	HA	60–70	(16–21)	2–3	Feb/Mar	
Cineraria maritima	HHA	65–75	(18–24)	2–3	Feb/Mar	
Clarkia	HA	60–75	(16–24)	1½–3	Apr	
Coleus	HHP	65–80	(18–27)	2½–4	Apr	
Cordyline	HHP	65–80	(18–27)	3–6	Jan/Feb	Soak seed for 24 hours. Erratic germination
Coreopsis	HP	60–70	(16–21)	2–4	Jan/Feb	
Cosmos	HHA	60–75	(16–24)	1½–2	Mar	
Crepis	HA	65–80	(18–27)	2–3	Mar	Barely cover seed
Dahlia	HHP	65–75	(18–24)	1½–2½	Apr	Grows quickly in warmth
Delphinium	HA	55–65	(13–18)	1½–2	Mar	Do not exceed 65°F (18°C)
Delphinium	HP	55–65	(13–18)	2–4	Jan	Sometimes erratic
Dimorphotheca	HHA	60–70	(16–21)	2–3	Mar/Apr	Barely cover seed
Eccremocarpus	HHA	65–70	(18–21)	4–10	Dec/Jan	Barely cover seed
Eschscholzia	HA	60–70	(16–21)	2–4	Mar	
Eucalyptus	HHP	70–80	(21–27)	2–12	Dec/Jan	
Euphorbia	HHA, HP	70–75	(21–24)	3–4	Feb/Mar	
Gaillardia	HHA	65–70	(18–21)	2–4	Feb/Mar	Do not cover seed
Gazania	HHA	65–80	(18–27)	2–3	Mar/Apr	
Geranium	HHP	70–75	(21–24)	1–1½	Jan	
Godetia	HA	60–70	(16–21)	1–2	Mar/Apr	
Gourds	HHA	75–80	(24–27)	2–4	Mar	Soak seed for 48 hours before sowing
Grasses	HA	55–70	(13–21)	2–3	Apr	Lightly cover seed
Gypsophila	HA, HP	60–70	(16–21)	2–3	Mar	Some perennials will flower first year from a January sowing
Helichrysum	HHA	65–80	(18–27)	1–2	Apr	Barely cover seed
Heliotrope	HHA	65–80	(18–27)	1–3	Mar/Apr	Slightly erratic
Herbs	HA, HP	55–70	(13–21)	1–4	Feb/Mar	
Hypoestes	HHA	65–80	(18–27)	1½–2	Mar/Apr	
Impatiens	HHA	70–75	(21–24)	2–3	Mar/Apr	Germinate in good light and high humidity
Ipomoea	HHA	70–80	(21–27)	1–3	Mar	Soak or chip seed before sowing
Kochia	HHA	65–75	(18–24)	1½–2	Apr	Surface sow
Lapageria	HHA	60–75	(16–24)	4–10	Jan	Soak seed for 2 hours. Use lime-free compost. Keep dark
Lavatera	HA	60–70	(16–21)	2–3	Mar	

SOWING TABLES

NAME	TYPE	TEMPERATURES °F	(°C)	TIME WEEKS	GERMINATION SOWING DATE	REMARKS
Limnanthes	HA	55–65	(13–18)	2–3	Mar	
Lobelia	HHA	65–80	(18–27)	1½–3	Feb	Surface sow
Lupin	HA	60–70	(16–21)	3–4	Mar	Sometimes erratic
Marigold	HHA	65–75	(18–24)	1–1½	Apr	
Matricaria	HHA	65–70	(18–21)	2–3		Surface sow
Matthiola	HB, HHA	55–70	(13–21)	1–2	Mar	Sow biennials in summer
Mesembryanthemum	HHA	65–70	(18–21)	2–3	Mar	Surface sow and germinate in darkness
Mimulus	HHA	65–70	(18–21)	2–3	Mar	Surface sow. Keep moist
Mina	HHA	65–75	(18–24)	4–6	Jan/Feb	Sow in individual pots
Molucella	HHA	65–80	(18–27)	2–3	Mar	Lightly cover seeds. Erratic
Myosotis	HB	65–70	(18–21)	2–3	June/July	Barely cover seeds
Nasturtium	HA	60–70	(16–21)	1½–3	Apr	
Nemesia	HHA	55–65	(13–18)	1½–3	Mar	Surface sow
Nemophila	HA	55–65	(13–18)	2–3	Mar	Do not exceed 65°F (18°C)
Nicotiana	HHA	65–80	(18–27)	1½–3	Mar/Apr	Barely cover seeds
Nigella	HA	66–75	(18–24)	1–2	Mar/Apr	Keep moist
Pansy	HP	65–75	(18–24)	2–3	Mar	Sow summer for spring flowers
Passiflora	HHP	65–80	(18–27)	6–12	Dec/Jan	Soak seed for 24 hours
Penstemon	HHA	70–80	(21–27)	2–5	Feb/Mar	
Petunia	HHA	70–80	(21–27)	2–3	Mar/Apr	Surface sow
Phacelia	HA	55–70	(13–21)	2–3	Mar	
Phlox	HHA	60–70	(16–21)	2–3	Mar	
Polyanthus & Primula	HP	55–65	(13–18)	3–5	May/Jun	Surface sow. Keep below 65°F (18°C)
Poppy	HA	55–65	(13–18)	2–3	Mar/Apr	
Portulaca	HHA	70–80	(21–27)	2–3	Mar	Lightly cover seeds
Pyrethrum	HHA	55–65	(13–18)	3–5	Feb/Mar	Sometimes erratic
Rhodochiton	HHA	60–70	(16–21)	2–6	Jan/Feb	Erratic germination
Ricinus	HHP	65–75	(18–24)	1–2	Apr	
Rudbeckia	HHA	70–80	(21–27)	1½–3	Mar/Apr	Lightly cover seed
Salpiglossis	HHA	65–80	(18–27)	2–4	Mar	Barely cover seed
Salvia	HHA	65–75	(16–24)	1–2	Apr	Lightly cover seed
Scabiosa	HA	60–75	(16–24)	1–3	Apr	
Schizanthus	HHA	60–70	(16–21)	2–3	Mar/Apr	Barely cover seed
Sweet Pea	HA	55–65	(13–18)	2–3	Feb/Mar	Chip those seeds which do not germinate
Swiss Chard	HA	55–65	(13–18)	1–3	Mar	
Tagetes	HHA	65–75	(18–24)	1–2	Apr	
Thunbergia	HHA	65–75	(18–24)	2–3	Mar	
Tithonia	HHA	70–80	(21–27)	1–2	Apr	
Tropaeolum peregrinum	HA	60–75	(16–24)	2–4	Feb/Mar	
Tropaeolum speciosum	HP	60–75	(16–24)	4–10	Dec/Jan	Seed needs chilling before warm sowing
Ursinia	HHA	55–70	(13–21)	2–3	Mar	Barely cover seed
Venidium	HHA	60–70	(16–21)	1–2	Apr	
Verbena	HHA	70–80	(21–27)	1½–3	Mar/Apr	Slightly erratic. Keep compost fairly dry
Vinca	HHA	65–75	(18–24)	2–3	Mar	
Viola	HP	65–75	(18–24)	2-3	Feb/Mar	
Wallflower	HB	65–75	(18–24)	1–2	Jun/Jul	
Xeranthemum	HA	55–70	(13–21)	1–2	Mar	
Zea	HHA	65–75	(18–24)	1–2	Apr	Better sown in individual pots
Zinnia	HHA	65–75	(18–24)	1–2	Apr	

3 • CULTIVATION

Even relative newcomers to gardening seem to be aware of the idea that bedding plants have a preference for poor soil. Like many myths, it contains an element of truth but is otherwise a misleading concept which denies the principles of plant growth. It is unquestionable that high levels of nitrogenous fertilizer will encourage an excess of foliage at the expense of flowers but this has little to do with soil fertility. All plants benefit from soil that is properly structured so that there is good drainage of superfluous water but also the retention of ample moisture. Sand drains too completely and clay can waterlog, but in between there is soil that drains well but retains sufficient moisture and has a proportion of decayed vegetable matter. Soil improvement should be the long-term aim and depends on the frequent addition of organic material, preferably incorporated during the winter.

Bedding plants are immensely popular and this implies that most gardeners have a successful show each year and are not discouraged by large-scale failure. While it is true that most bedding subjects are resilient when faced by a variety of soil conditions, the visual rewards will be much greater if the groundwork is done. Plants in a very hot, dry summer will desiccate if the soil is light and sandy and those in a heavy clay will literally drown in a wet season. The structure of the soil is of paramount importance whereas the presence or otherwise of fertilizer should be of marginal concern; if nutrients become necessary, they are easily and quickly added.

Preparation

A couple of weeks before planting, the soil should be raked and generally tidied, and obvious weeds removed. Even in a fertile garden, it is prudent to apply a dressing of a balanced plant food at a rate of about 60g (2oz) to the square metre (although you

Heliotrope This genus offers a surprising lack of variety but 'Marine' provides everything that a gardener could wish for — superb foliage, a tidy habit of growth, pretty clusters of bloom and a delicious fragrance.

should always follow the manufacturer's instructions).

The plants, too, will need some preparatory attention and home-raised bedding must have spent a week or so outdoors to acclimatize to the cooler conditions. Ready-to-plant material may have been hardened off before sale but it is wise to assume that this is not so. Buy the plants about a week before the proposed planting date and keep them in their trays placed close to a south-facing wall of the house.

Planting

The first decision concerns the date of

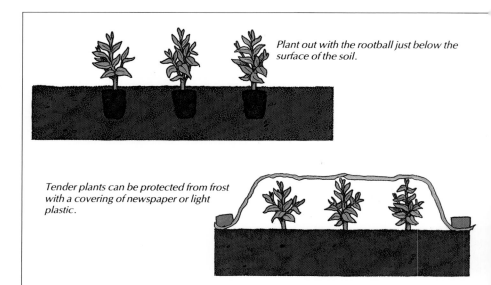

Plant out with the rootball just below the surface of the soil.

Tender plants can be protected from frost with a covering of newspaper or light plastic.

Plants that have grown together should not be pulled apart – use a breadknife and ensure that each has a portion of roots.

planting and this obviously depends on personal factors, but for summer bedding the timing can be crucial. Of course, the best time is after the last frost has occurred but sadly, this date is only known in retrospect! If the forecasts are favourable then the opportunity must be taken but beware any impending high-pressure weather which can often bring late frosts.

If you are working to a plan, ensure that this is clear in your mind and that areas in the garden have been marked out if necessary. Pegs and string will be helpful when straight lines are desired but otherwise only a trowel and a watering can are needed. The plants should be watered well about an hour before planting begins so that they will not be stressed by a few dry days.

If the plants are in individual containers, planting is swift and pleasurable but those in open trays will present the irritating problem of separating roots. It may be possible to tease the plants apart but time and patience will be saved if a knife is used from the start.

The next aim is to plant at the correct depth: the uppermost parts of the rooting system must be just below ground level. Unless the plants are from large pots, the trowel will remove sufficient soil in one operation and progress is quickly made but the plants must be handled with care. Some leaf damage is tolerable but broken stems, especially low down, can be serious or even fatal. When the soil has been returned around the rootball, it should be firmed with the fingers (not with feet!)

Catalogues or seed packets indicate how far apart the plants should be positioned but many gardeners have their own views. It is visually more satisfactory for plants to just touch each other when they are mature and it also leaves the minimum of bare soil which can be invaded by weeds. Experience is the best aid to judgement about planting distances, which obviously vary with different types of bedding, but novice

Plants grown in individual compartments are conveniently handled.

gardeners should begin their careers by erring on the close side.

Watering is the last act of planting and should be carried out even if the soil is judged to be adequately moist. Overhead watering is helpful because it settles the plant in position and washes soil into the spaces which would otherwise exist around the roots. If there is no appreciable rainfall within a week of planting, it will be necessary to use the watering can again, treating each plant individually.

The worst thing that can happen after planting is frost and if this is predicted, there are two options: you can take the risk that the soil is sufficiently warm to protect the plants from all but slight damage, or you can use a covering. Sheet plastic or newspaper provide quick shelter although sceptics may doubt the efficacy of such measures because even a light wind would remove the protection. However, the presence of wind would almost certainly preclude the possibility of a damaging ground frost.

One final point: it is worth taking precautions against the possibility that some of the plants may fail. The best way of doing this is to put two or three of each type of plant used in the display into 9cm (3½in) or 10cm (4in) pots. If the odd failure does occur then replacement is a simple matter; if every single plant succeeds then you will have some delightful pot plants with which to decorate the greenhouse, conservatory or a sunny windowsill in the house.

Maintaining the Display

After the initial settling-in period, when a lack of rain must always bring the watering can into use, the plants will have become established and will be able to resist periods of unfavourable weather. However, although some bedding subjects can cope with long spells of drought, there are others that will deteriorate or even succumb altogether. In these circumstances, watering 'little but often' is futile and the rule is to irrigate occasionally but thoroughly. Inattention to watering can lead to a foreshortened display, even fatal consequences.

Most modern bedding plants have been bred to produce bushy growth with numerous stems emerging to carry flowers. Sometimes, because of inferior cultivation, the plants are 'leggy' with elongated and sparse growth. If this is apparent, the top 2cm of the stems should be 'pinched out' to promote a more satisfactory habit. Some gardeners practise the technique with all young plants but it is not often necessary and will delay the initial flowers.

It is widely believed that removing the faded flowers is an act of extreme tidiness practised by fastidious gardeners. However, the more important reason is that taking off the developing seed pods perverts the

Pinching out the growing tip will encourage bushy growth but most of the modern generation of compact bedding plants do not require this treatment.

plant's primary intentions and prompts the production of more flowers. Examples like *Impatiens* and *Begonia semperflorens* require no such treatment as they are 'self-cleaning': the expired blooms fall off naturally and the seed heads drop, usually, before they have developed. *Ageratum, Lobelia* and *Alyssum* pose a very labour-intensive task and the effort is hardly worthwhile but with most subjects, it is highly effective in prolonging their flowering season.

As the summer progresses, it is inevitable that some weed seeds will find their way to vacant ground and their growth is a source of irritation for all gardeners. If the earlier advice on planting distances is taken, the unoccupied areas will be few. Wide open spaces invite invasion. Many gardeners resort to the hoe but it is difficult to negotiate flower beds without damaging wanted plants. Even if a hoe can be used safely, it requires a dry soil and the absence of rain for a few days otherwise the weeds are merely moved from one place to another where they easily root again. The most effective though least attractive method, is hand weeding which does involve a lot of bending or kneeling.

The maintenance of a bedding display is not arduous but, like other aspects of gardening, it is most successfully achieved with regular bouts of attention. Spending ten minutes each week in weeding and deadheading is significantly more efficient than devoting forty minutes every month to intensive activity. Four-week-old weeds are larger and more tenacious than one-week old ones, and a month's accumulation of faded flowers can be overfacing.

If the weather is consistently dry, do not neglect the watering. The only other job is to apply another dressing of fertilizer over the flower beds – about eight weeks after planting – which will invigorate the plants until the end of their season.

Cuttings should be taken directly below a leaf joint. The base should be dipped in rooting powder before planting the cutting in compost.

Taking Cuttings

While not a principal means of raising plants for the bedding display, because of the numerous stock plants which would be needed, taking cuttings is a useful method of propagating individual plants which have extra appeal. Seed-raised plants are always variable, if only slightly, but cuttings produce a result which is identical to the parent. Cuttings can be taken from the leaves or roots of some species but the most common are those from stems.

Cut the top few inches from a growing shoot, preferably one without flowers or buds, at a point immediately below a leaf joint. The bottom leaves and their stalks should be removed leaving the growing tip and at least one pair of leaves intact. The cut end is inserted into a pot containing fresh compost and the cutting is gently watered, after which it can be placed in a propagator or enclosed in a plastic bag. This is important otherwise the shoot would quickly lose moisture and die before roots had the time to form. The propagator or plastic 'tent' must be kept out of direct sunshine to prevent the consequent over-heating. Hormone rooting powders are a useful aid because they also contain a fungicide which protects the severed stem from the ingress of disease. It would be pointless to take cuttings of true annual subjects but *impatiens*, begonias, fuchsias and geraniums are excellent examples of plants which root easily during spring and late summer, and there are many others which are suitable.

4 • DESIGN CONSIDERATIONS

Many of the permanent plants in the garden are grown for the variety of shape that is offered by their outline and often for the textural effect of foliage. Bedding plants do provide contrasts in shape and texture but their principal role is to provide colour that is pleasing to the eye, usually from flowers but sometimes from leaves. For many gardeners, this is the most important feature but the effect of colour does change according to the overall and local context.

Conventionally, the colours of 'Aurora Fire' marigolds and Ageratum 'Blue Champion' do not combine well.

Colour

There are some unwritten rules about colour arrangements – 'Pink does not associate well with orange, and red alongside blue is an assault on the retina' – and many people will not wish to risk infringement. However, the consequence of breaking rules can be a spectacular display and many unorthodox colour schemes achieve great success.

Basically, colours harmonize well with those that are in the same part of the spectrum and contrast with those that are further removed. A bold approach using strong colours can be too striking – at least in theory – but since various shades of green are an integral part of most plants, the violent contrast is softened. It is 'safer' to use pastel shades and current trends seem to point in this direction. However, the effect of weather must be taken into account because the popular pastels appear almost colourless in strong sunshine and become almost luminous in the shade or on overcast days. Another characteristic of the colour spectrum is that one half gives a warm and bright effect – from yellow through orange to red and crimson – while the greens and blues have a muted appearance which can be described as cool.

Geraniums in mixed colours planted about 23cm (9in) apart.

Single-colour or Multi-colour Arrangements

Large gardens do present an opportunity for devoting one area to a single colour and the result is pleasing but domestic gardeners rarely adopt this policy. White is a possibility for any size of garden and gives a restful impression but the majority of gardeners opt for much greater diversity. One system which does work on a small or large scale is to use a wide variety of plants of different shades and tints of the same basic colour. Petunias, geraniums, *impatiens*, begonias and antirrhinums, for instance, are available in shades of pink and a single colour gives a sense of unity to plants that are otherwise quite different (in height, foliage and habit of growth).

Sales figures of bedding plants show that a mixture of colours is the popular choice; packet seed is also more popular in mixed colours. A look in most gardens confirms that the favoured display comprises the widest possible colour range, but this can look rather confused. What does help is the addition of another element which will help to blend widely different colours. This is pleasingly achieved with so called 'dot' plants, either in small groups or singly, placed amongst the kaleidoscopic scene. A number of subjects are suitable but the silver foliage of *Cineraria maritima* and the similar *Pyrethrum ptarmicaeflorum* are excellent and frequently used examples.

In Bakewell town centre, colourful petunias are contrasted with tall dot plants – kochia.

Professional designers favour the silver-leaved Cineraria maritima, *seen here as an edging plant at Springfields Gardens.*

The question of colour is further complicated by the influence of fashion, but where gardening is concerned personal preference should always prevail. Mistakes may be made but they are unlikely to be serious and the joy of bedding is that it is only there for a season. Next time, the whole plan can be changed; the canvas is clear for another attempt to satisfy personal tastes.

Formal Bedding

The choice of colours is dependent to some extent on what planting scheme is adopted

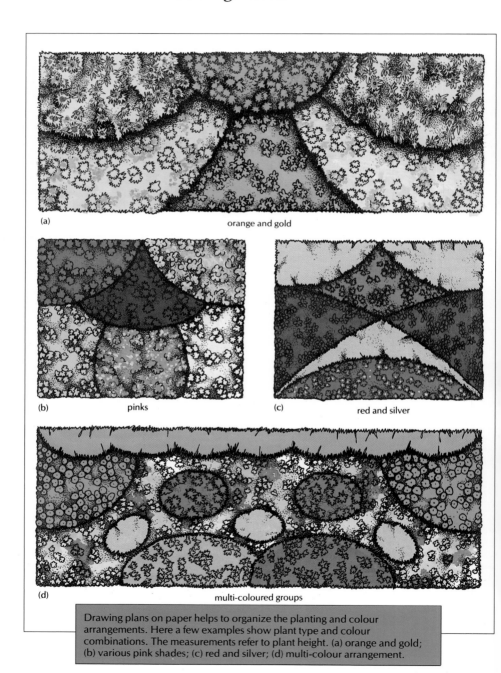

(a) orange and gold

(b) pinks

(c) red and silver

(d) multi-coloured groups

Drawing plans on paper helps to organize the planting and colour arrangements. Here a few examples show plant type and colour combinations. The measurements refer to plant height. (a) orange and gold; (b) various pink shades; (c) red and silver; (d) multi-colour arrangement.

and although formal arrangements are on the decline, they represent the zenith of traditional bedding. Parks and public gardens exemplify the formal plan, usually embracing strict geometric shapes. Where beds can be viewed from all directions, they typically use taller plants in the centre with smaller ones around and dwarf edging subjects on the perimeter. In borders, taller specimens dominate the rear and shorter plants are arranged progressively towards the front. Beds and borders also incorporate dot plants, either foliage or flowering, and these are placed according to geometric rules.

Smaller gardens need taller plants for variety; in this case, Rudbeckia, Lavatera *and standard fuchsias are used.*

A scale drawing of the garden is most helpful in allocating space to various subjects. It also helps you to visualize a new design and make necessary adjustments before you are committed to it for the summer.

Considerable expertise is necessary for formal schemes where the aim is to have every plant flowering at the same time, and uniformity of height is essential amongst the different bedding elements. Individual plant failures are immediately apparent and replacements must always be grown to perpetuate the splendid symmetry. These factors are a disincentive for most home gardeners but it is also unlikely that the average garden has beds and borders that do not contain other, permanent plants. If a bed is used solely for bedding, it will be bare during the winter unless steps are taken to introduce another scheme.

Informal Schemes

Beds and borders can also be planted in more carefree fashion and this means that permanent plants like shrubs and flowering

Close planting makes an effective display.

because they prevail in suburban situations and at some times of the year, the bushes reveal how unattractive they can be. If the roses are underplanted with spring and, later, summer bedding plants, the naked stems can be masked from view or at least the groundwork flowers will distract the eye from painful sights.

Infill Planting

The last decade or so has witnessed the emergence of the low-maintenance garden where trouble-free flowering or foliage shrubs are the dominant feature together with the occasional tree and group of perennial flowers. This permanent frame-

Close planting and uniformity of height is relieved with occasional dot plants; the main subjects are 'Non-Stop' begonias, tagetes and marigolds.

perennials can be included in the overall plan. It is not necessary for all the plants to bloom simultaneously and the display will depend on irregularity as its theme. Some pattern can prevail but the whole essence is to use a variety of plants to complement each other and to express your gardening flair. Plants can be added or removed at any time without spoiling the show and, properly arranged, there can be a progressive transition from one season to the next. Rose beds deserve special mention in this context work occupies a large proportion of the cultivated ground but is a perfect foil for colourful bedding plants. One simple strategy is to introduce a miscellany of these temporary subjects wherever space allows but the visual impact is heightened if due forethought has been given to colour. Groups comprising three or four of the same kind of plant, with similarly coloured flowers, give the best result with the odd foliage subject to add balance. Rose beds, as mentioned earlier, are very suitable for infilling but rockeries and shrubberies will also benefit and the only precaution is to avoid using tall bedders that are out of scale with the permanent occupants of the garden. Clearly, where this system is used in a newly created garden, the spaces between the permanent plants will decrease annually as the shrubs and perennials increase in size.

Other Bedding Systems

The first which should be mentioned, although it is not presently in favour with domestic gardens, is carpet bedding. Traditionally, dwarf plants were used whose colours derived from leaves; flowering subjects were rarely planted. This made it possible to make detailed portrayals of coats of arms, other insignia and some famous clocks. Flower buds and wayward stems were removed to maintain a regular outline and frequent trimming of the leaves was necessary. Some examples, especially of the clocks, can still be seen in public parks and gardens but the modern exponents of the art often use miniature flowering plants. Genera such as *Alternatha*, *Echeveria* and *Sagina* were the mainstays of carpet bedding; these became quite uncommon but recently there has been renewed interest and some commercial growers can supply suitable plants.

Raised beds are not really an alternative

The dot plants in this Southport public garden are cannas with pink geraniums providing the main colour.

bedding system but they do allow an otherwise flat garden to be enhanced by an added dimension. All the bedding schemes are appropriate for higher level treatment but the great advantage is that smaller or pendulous flowers are better appreciated when they are closer to eye level. If there are no raised areas in the garden then some construction work is inevitable but it is easily accomplished by the competent DIY enthusiast. The project does not require

Petunia A bed of petunias is probably the most colourful part of the garden but some are so vivid that companion shades should be selected with care. Perhaps the most surprising fact is that despite their delicate appearance, these flowers are robust, even in rain.

painstaking accuracy and bricks or stone blocks are easily laid to a satisfactory standard. An advisable minimum width is perhaps four bricks (about 90cm – 3ft), with a height of at least four courses giving approximately 50cm (20in). Such a bed is a delight to plant and its upkeep is very convenient.

Design Summary

Every garden is unique and the possible combinations of permanent plants mean that it is unrealistic to offer specific advice.

Gardeners should indulge their own tastes, even in the face of general guidelines that advise differently on the various schemes and the use of colour. Some spirit of adventure is desirable and will involve changes from one year to the next because only a degree of experimentation will enable the gardener to realize what pleases most. Growing hitherto unknown bedding plants and embarking on an innovative plan is part of the excitement, and the consequent gain in experience is invaluable. For those who face planning a garden for the first time – and even for regular practitioners – it is always helpful to look elsewhere for inspiration.

There is no shortage of imaginative bedding displays in local parks and gardens, and tourist towns place considerable emphasis on bedding schemes in parks and around public buildings. Fleuroselect is a European organization established by major plant breeders and devoted to bringing the merits of outstanding plants before the public, so it is worth visiting the gardens that are host to Fleuroselect varieties. New varieties are trialled at twenty sites in Europe, and prize-winners must perform well in southern Italy and Finland, and at the places in between. They must possess qualities such as a lengthy flowering period and blooms that are likely to appeal to most gardeners. Fleuroselect is not a comprehensive guide to noteworthy plants, but their award winners are usually superb varieties that are well worth seeing. Springfields Gardens were set up by the commercial bulb growers of Lincolnshire as a showplace for their produce. Some years ago a bedding plant enterprise began and Springfields has become the most important show place in Britain for bedding plants. It is well worth a visit. Many of the large seed companies also have their own displays which are open to the public at certain times. The gardening press is a useful source of information on venues to visit.

5 • CONTAINER BEDDING

It is not surprising that container gardening is so popular: it enhances hard-surface areas like paths and patios and also enables flat dwellers and those without gardens to enjoy the delights of living with plants. Apart from the obvious limitation of physical size, virtually any plant can be successfully cultivated.

Tubs

Stone is the most desirable material for tubs but few are manufactured these days and those that are in existence are prized items and rarely offered for sale. Reconstituted stone is an option and many examples replicate their priceless predecessors but the cost is usually high. Concrete is the practical alternative and those with simple designs are the most convincing, although the initial appearance is rather stark. However, the weathering process and colonization by lichens and mosses soon soften the rude newness. Stone and concrete are extremely heavy and this is a disadvantage where regular changes of site are anticipated. Otherwise the weight is

Primrose *Primula*   Spring would not be the same without the charming and reliable primroses but it is vital to choose hardy varieties for the garden because many types have been bred as pot plants and will succumb to frosty weather.

highly desirable because it offers complete stability.

Plastic is derided by many gardeners as an unsympathetic material but the better-quality items are inoffensive and immensely practical. Ultimately, they do deteriorate and then will crack and disintegrate but their cost is such that replacement is not financially punishing. Fibreglass is an alternative which is very durable but the price is often a deterrent and this material shares with plastic the deficiency of light weight and hence instability especially when they are filled with the peat-based composts.

The natural look of wood is compatible with a garden setting and is sufficiently substantial to offer reasonable stability. Decay can be a problem but an annual treatment with preservative will postpone

Cascade petunias succeed in any sunny situation.

deterioration almost indefinitely. It is also possible to use a plastic pot within the wooden container to separate the soil from the interior surface.

Terracotta is a popular choice which offers some beautiful designs but the material is fragile and breakages are always possible. In addition, many such pots are not frost-proof and after a few winters, flaking and cracking may occur.

plastic

concrete

reconstituted stone

fibreglass

wood

terracotta

Many different materials are used for garden containers.

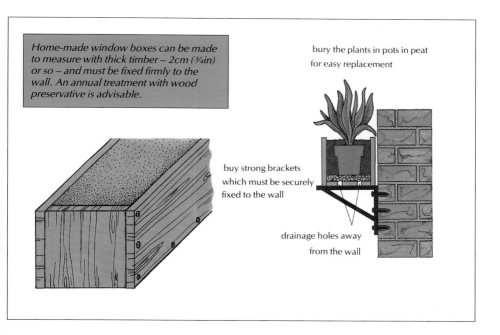

Home-made window boxes can be made to measure with thick timber – 2cm (¾in) or so – and must be fixed firmly to the wall. An annual treatment with wood preservative is advisable.

bury the plants in pots in peat for easy replacement

buy strong brackets which must be securely fixed to the wall

drainage holes away from the wall

Window-Boxes

There is little argument about the aesthetic appeal of window-boxes, but they have fallen out of favour because of the difficulties of fixing them. Considerable weight is involved and strong, metal brackets must be firmly fixed to the wall. Plastic boxes are easily obtained but the dimensions may present a problem if a perfect match is required for the window. Wooden boxes can be constructed at home, without great skill, with the advantage that they can be made to measure. Sturdy boxes are essential to contain large volumes of compost which becomes very heavy when watered. Conventional planting is the norm but a more versatile arrangement is the use of potted plants, surrounded by compost, which can be conveniently replaced at any time.

Spring colour in a window-box provided by pansies and Alyssum saxatile.

Hanging Baskets

Wire baskets are chosen by the purists but many gardeners are daunted by the

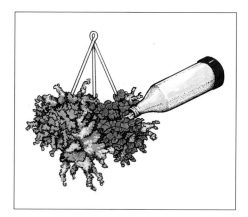

There are some patented devices for lowering hanging baskets for watering but otherwise a plastic bottle is easily manipulated at arm's length.

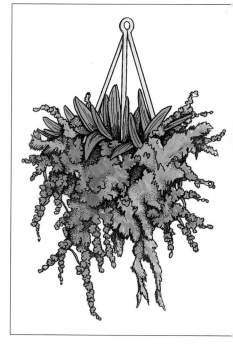

A hanging basket that relies on foliage plants is unusual and attractive.

prospect of lining them with moss or by the outrageous price which is often charged for the moss. It is possible to use plastic sheet as a liner, with holes cut for drainage and to accommodate plants at the sides, but the initial result is not aesthetically pleasing. Subsequent growth eventually masks the offending material but there are also fibre liners which look more agreeable and will last for some years. On the other hand, there are numerous basket designs in plastic which are essentially practical and some are visually attractive. Different colours are offered and many have an attached 'saucer' which is a useful reservoir to reduce the frequency of watering. The main consideration is a basket with sufficient depth to contain enough compost to allow plants to prosper.

Container Maintenance

When growing plants in any container, the most irksome task is ensuring that moisture needs are supplied, particularly in hot summers; this involves considerable attention. If potting composts are used, there will be ample reserves of water in the early stages but as the plants grow, needs increase dramatically. It is an unfortunate but inevitable consequence of enjoying container gardens that they require dedication and selfless application. Even on days when there is some rainfall, mature plantings will almost surely need additional watering. It is possible to arrange drips from a perforated hosepipe which can water numerous containers from an outside tap that is left on permanently. However, it is an obtrusive arrangement and may only be considered for periods when you are away on holiday.

Not only does the density of planting

exacerbate the need for frequent watering, it also leads to rapid depletion of nutrients in the compost. This is especially true in the limited root space in hanging baskets but all container plants should be fed regularly. Since watering is frequent, it is little extra trouble to add a liquid fertilizer, at weekly intervals, and at the recommended rate of dilution.

Otherwise, the only other regular task is ensuring that flowers are deadheaded and that damaged or dead leaves are removed. If a plant fails completely or deteriorates prematurely, it should be pulled out and replaced by using a knife to cut into the compost if this seems necessary. A handful of fresh compost and a new plant will quickly restore the display.

Plectranthus Foliage plants can make a substantial contribution to the success of a bedding display. They are also useful in tubs and hanging baskets and the variegated *Plectranthus* makes an attractive pot plant.

Choice of Plants

There is no reason why any plant should not flourish in a container and the choice will reflect individual preferences but aesthetics demand that the size of the occupant is in proportion with the tub or basket. Flowers will commonly dominate the arrangements but every display is improved by the inclusion of one or two foliage subjects. Indeed, a display that is exclusively planted for foliar effect is rather unusual, easily maintained and pleasing. The only important difference between flowering plants is that some require long periods exposed to direct sunlight and some perform well in shaded positions. In the latter case, selection should be made from plants such as begonia, fuchsia, *impatiens*, mimulus, nicotiana, pansies and violas.

It is noticeable that most containers are neglected in winter, although it is quite feasible to have a display throughout the year. Replanting can take place in late autumn using, for example, evergreens like dwarf conifers, euonymus, heathers and ivy together with winter-flowering pansies, primulas and polyanthus. Adding a few spring bulbs will ensure an attractive show which is some compensation for the period when the garden may be bleak and featureless.

One last thought on containers which, so far, has not been explored in many gardens is the possibility of creating vertical bedding. It involves the use of improvised containers which can be stacked upon each other to the required height. Something like milk crates is ideal and there are a number of other plastic containers which are used in everyday life, which could easily be converted for gardening use. In some cases, the sides would need lining to contain the compost but the results are novel and attractive and may be the only direction for enthusiastic gardeners to go when the horizontal space is filled but the ambitions for expansion persist.

6 • PLANT CATEGORIES

Plants are categorized to help gardeners identify how suitable they are for various purposes and to give an indication of the plant's life cycle. The plant names listed on pages 39–57 have been followed by an abbreviation to suggest how they are best grown for bedding but this may contradict the precise description of their natural characteristics. For instance, antirrhinum and wallflowers are perennial by nature but after their first flowering season, the plants are past their best and do not merit permanent occupancy of the garden; therefore, they are better grown as annuals and discarded after the first year. Other perennials like *impatiens* and gazania need winter protection to survive so they, too, are grown as annuals and thrown away after their first season. Similarly, biennial plants may survive for subsequent years but their quality deteriorates, so it is better to discard them when their first display is over. It is also noteworthy that a few subjects may fall into more than one category.

Hardy Annuals (HA)
A hardy annual is a plant that can resist quite low temperatures and may be sown outdoors, generally in the spring. They grow, flower, and then set seed in the same year, after which they die.

Half-Hardy Annuals (HHA)
The seed of these subjects requires warm conditions to germinate and the plants will not withstand frost. Like hardy annuals they grow, flower and produce seed within the same year but many in this category are actually perennial and will live from year to year if suitably protected in the winter.

Hardy Biennials (HB)
Hardy biennial plants are usually sown in late spring or summer, after which they grow leaves and stems. Being hardy, they live through winter and then flower in the following spring or summer and then die.

Hardy Perennials (HP)
Such plants can live for many years and although in most cases the vegetation dies down in winter, new leaves and stems emerge each spring, followed by the flowers.

Half-Hardy Perennials (HHP)
Half-hardy perennials are often a tropical or sub-tropical subject; they will be killed by frost and need to be cultivated in a greenhouse or conservatory during the coldest months. Catalogues often classify these plants as GP (greenhouse perennials).

Half-Hardy Shrubs (HHS)
The definition of shrub is vague and many catalogues describe these plants as hardy perennials. Strictly, a shrub develops so that the lower and older stems become woody although the upper parts may be soft and green, but this depends on the plant's age and site. Geraniums in bedding displays are recognized as diminutive plants with soft, green stems but visitors to Mediterranean countries or other areas of similar climate will have seen that the geranium is very much a shrub in its natural conditions.

F_1 Hybrids
Catalogues list numerous varieties of seed, which is produced from two inbred plants: one provides the pollen while the other produces the seed. The process usually involves hand pollination which is painstaking and laborious and consequently, F_1 seed is expensive. The resultant plants are more vigorous, more disease-resistant and very even in colour and form.

Open-Pollinated Varieties
Most seed results from growing the parent plants in a field situation where pollination occurs by natural means. The parents are selected, each year, to ensure that the offspring maintains the essential characteristics and, if inferior plants are removed, the seed quality is gradually improved.

7• THE SPRING DISPLAY

A beautiful summer show in the garden is the priority in most cases but the opportunities for spring bedding displays should not be ignored even though mass displays of colour can present more difficulties than are usually encountered in an average cultivated plot. Again, public parks are the custodians of the most memorable early collections of horticultural colour. In most parks, bulbs form the main component; tulips are usually the favourite but daffodils, grape hyacinths and crocus are usually included. There are some bedding plants that can be interplanted with the bulbs but the choice is much more limited than that which prevails in the summer. Some are perennial and can be saved for the future while others have a shorter life and will be destined for the compost heap but whatever the selection, home gardeners can rarely

Tulip beds in Stamford Park, Ashton under Lyne. In parks, tulips often stand unaccompanied but in a garden, they look better underplanted with short plants.

Godetia Undoubtedly one of the old favourites, godetias have great charm but they should be planted close together otherwise they sprawl rather badly. Plants grow easily and quickly from seed and bloom for about six to eight weeks. 'Salmon Princess', shown here, is a superb example.

emulate the parks' practices: there is insufficient space to store the out of season perennial plants and, except in the very largest gardens, spare beds are unheard of. Leaving the bulbs in the ground is not entirely satisfactory because tulips require a drying off period which is not often scheduled in British or other unreliable climates and their subsequent performance is strongly linked to warm, dry storage. On the other hand, daffodils and crocus are so successful, and expand so much, that there is little room to insert a trowel to plant the summer bedding. There is also the problem of dying foliage which mars the garden's appearance in early summer.

Probably the best compromise in domestic gardens is to have small groups of spring flowers dotted around rather than to concentrate them *en masse*. In this way, bulbs can be left to die off without greatly affecting the overall scene and spring plants are soon masked by the summer bedding. This enables a transition between the seasons without upheaval or untidiness and separate storage areas are not needed for saving the spring-flowering perennials.

Spring Plants

The plants under this heading and those in later chapters are listed under their Latin names except where the common name is universally acknowledged. This does cause some confusion but some plants have no popular name and others have a botanical name which is too unfamiliar for everyday use. An abbreviated classification accompanies each plant which describes how the plants are usually grown for bedding purposes and newcomers to gardening should consult Chapter 6 (*see* page 38) if there is uncertainty about the meaning of any of the abbreviations or other terms.

Alyssum saxatile   HP
This is most usually grown as a rockery subject but it is reliable in most situations. Plants are widely available and numerous seed strains are offered in various shades of yellow.

Alyssum saxatile *is usually found in rockeries but it is suitable for beds.*

Arabis (Rock Cress)   HP
An excellent low-growing perennial, usually with white flowers, but pink strains are available from seed. It has a slightly invasive habit but it is not difficult to contain.

Aubretia   HP
Mostly used as a cascading subject, this plant is highly effective on level ground. The flowers are typically in blue shades but pinks and reds can also be raised from seed.

Aubretia *is also happy cascading or on the flat.*

Auricula   HP
A member of the primula family, this was at one time highly prized as a show flower. Only a limited range of seed varieties are available and plants are rarely offered.

Bellis perennis   HP
Basically there are two kinds: one that grows to about 15cm (6in) and has button-sized flowers; and one that grows to twice the height and has much larger flowers. Colours are confined to various shades of red, pink and white. Plants are widely sold and many seed strains are catalogued.

Forget-Me-Not (*Myosotis*)   HB
Height varies from 15–45cm (6–18in). Most usually the flowers are blue, but there are also white and pink varieties. The loose habit of the taller kinds combines well with

summer sowing is necessary for flowering the following spring.

Polyanthus HP

This is one of the primula group of plants. It flowers over a very long period and is easily cared for when in a moist position with some protection from summer sunshine. The 'Pacific Giants' are long established but are not as reliable as the F_1 'Crescendo' which is a superb bedding plant. The polyanthus is indistinguishable from the primrose except that its blooms are borne in clusters whereas primroses have one flower per stem. Seed should be sown in May or June but germination is not always easy; permanent moisture and surface sowing are essential, as is a temperature that is kept below 18°C (65°C).

The 'Crescendo' series of polyanthus has a wide colour range which includes a lovely cream with a yellow centre.

Bellis perennis is a long-flowered spring flower.

the upright nature of bulbs like tulips and daffodils.

Pansy HA, HB, HP

A versatile plant which, depending on the sowing time and variety, can provide flowers almost every month of the year. The Universal strain has become famous for its ability to flower in mild winters and is available in a large range of colours. Universals are F_1 hybrids and thus expensive but 'Floral Dance' is a cheaper alternative for winter and early spring colour. Early

Pansies are superb performers and are available in an enormous colour range.

Primrose (*Primula*) HP

Most modern primroses have been bred for indoor pot use and are not winter hardy but the variety 'Husky' is reliable in this respect. The species *Primula denticulata* (the drumstick primrose), and the common primrose *P. vulgaris* are perfectly robust and so too

Stocks *Matthiola* For an old-fashioned show, there is little to rival stocks and although the flowering period is not prolonged, they offer something that is quite rare amongst modern bedding plants: a superb scent.

Viola (Violet)   HP

It is difficult to distinguish between violas and pansies because the latter have been bred from the former, but two differences are apparent. Violas have smaller flowers and are invariably more hardy than their larger relations. Most plants and seed are sold as mixed colours but separate colours like the deep purple 'Prince Henry' and 'Yellow Prince' are available. Perhaps the most appealing are those with little 'faces' such as the variety 'Bambini'.

Wallflower (*Cheiranthus*)   HB

This is the backbone plant for massed colour but raising them from seed is necessary for a quality show. Commercially grown plants are offered in autumn but they are often grown in fields and uprooted by machine resulting in large plants with small root systems. Seed is inexpensive and wallflowers grow easily. They should be transplanted in autumn.

Wallflowers look attractive in both single colours and combinations.

are the candelabras, *P. japonica*, which grow to about 45cm (18in). Primula seed can be difficult to raise but the plants are easily propagated by division.

Stocks (*Matthiola*)   HB

Nowadays, stocks are almost a rarity in domestic gardens but their beauty and delicious fragrance demand attention. The main problem is the confusion over different varieties and although they are classed as hardy, some protection is desirable during the winter. The Brompton stocks are used for spring and they should be sown in May or June and, ideally, grown in frames and planted out at the end of February.

8 • THE SUMMER DISPLAY

The Top Performers

Disregarding, for a moment, the gardener's personal taste in summer flowers, there are some subjects which deserve serious consideration because they offer the major characteristics that are desired: a long-lasting display; mass colour impact; resistance to adverse conditions.

There is no perfect bedding plant but those listed below are contenders for the title and satisfy all the principal, functional criteria to a greater or lesser extent. There is no doubt about their performance and they can constitute the main, or even sole component, of a summer show but obviously it is important to decide whether they are aesthetically pleasing to you.

The bronze foliage of Begonia *'Light Pink Devil' combines well with African marigolds and* Rudbeckia.

Begonia semperflorens
(Fibrous-rooted Begonia)   HHA

This is the supreme edging and dwarf bedding subject with a very compact habit, pretty foliage in green or shades of bronze, and continuous flowers until the first major frost. It is also tolerant of some shade and dry conditions and performs well in a wet summer, but the colour range is confined to white and a few shades of pink and red. Some strains offer larger flowers on plants which reach about 30cm (12in) in height but those most commonly purchased are 15–20cm (6–8in) tall and include 'Organdy', 'Cocktail' and the 'Devil' series. Surprisingly, the major award institutions have not honoured *B. semperflorens* on many occasions, but many of the national display gardens depend on its reliable performance. The plants are fairly expensive and this reflects the fact that the seed must be sown in January and February for flowering towards the end of May. The seed is minute, presenting some sowing difficulties and the young plants grow rather slowly although greenhouse and conservatory owners should expect success. The seed is sown on the surface of the compost and the tray must be kept in a propagator or within a plastic bag, in light conditions and at an optimum temperature of 18–21°C (65–75°F). Moisture is critical for such small seeds and seedlings until they reach the size when pricking out is necessary.

Begonia
(Tuberous-rooted Begonia)   HHP

The large-flowered begonias are often grown as tub or hanging basket subjects but some types are very suitable for garden beds and are perhaps the most glamorous of all bedding. Unfortunately, they are expensive but there is the advantage that the tubers can be saved from year to year and, gradually, a modest annual expenditure can lead to a useful collection of supreme plants. They can be grown from seed but the seedlings need supplementary light otherwise they will not mature until midsummer. From seed or as plants or tubers, the most highly acclaimed strain is 'Non Stop' which provides magnificent, double flowers in yellow, red, orange, pink, apricot and white, and most attractive foliage. The plants are prone to drought and some

Begonia *'Non-Stop' has become one of the classic bedding plants.*

all bedding plants in the United States and in Britain because its merits are incomparable. Performance is marred by persistent dry weather but if the soil is kept moist, the plants flower ceaselessly and the colour range is extensive. These plants are also excellent in shade although really murky conditions will reduce the flowering potential. Two strains have dominated for many years: 'Accent' and 'Super Elfin'. 'Accent' is always more expensive but few gardeners will be disappointed with 'Super Elfin', 'Novette' and 'Sparkles'.

Recent years have seen the development of the New Guinea hybrids, which have notable foliage, often bronze or variegated, but the high price of plants has determined their main use as pot or tub subjects. One

watering will be essential in a hot, dry summer otherwise the results will be inferior. If the tubers are stored in dry peat with protection from frost they will survive the winter. Cuttings can then be taken in the spring, and the tubers can be planted again.

The New Guinea hybrid impatiens *are presently too expensive for planting* en masse *but they are ideal for tubs.*

Busy Lizzie (*Impatiens*)   HHA

Impatiens has become the most popular of

Busy Lizzie *Impatiens*   The renowned pastel shades of the humble Busy Lizzie have helped to make it the most important of all bedding plants. It satisfies the requirement for long-lasting colour in a variety of situations and weather conditions.

variety 'Tango', is available from seed and has huge orange flowers, while the 'Spectre' strain offers mixed flower colours together with varied foliage. All *impatiens* seed germinates readily at 21°C (70°F) but the seedlings can be awkward to manage in cool, dull conditions. Home raisers should delay sowing until towards the end of March.

French Marigold   HHA

There is some disregard among many gardeners for these plants but they have admirable characteristics. Flowering is throughout the summer and they are not daunted by wet weather, but it is true that the colours are confined to the yellows and oranges with some red tinting. The flowers can be single, semi-double or fully double, and there is a huge choice of varieties. The Afro-French varieties are equally compact in their growth but their flowers rival those of the African Marigolds for size.

Seed is best sown in April because it germinates rapidly and the plants grow quickly and without fuss. Varieties like 'Aurora', 'Boy' and 'Alamo' are certain to please and, of the Afro-French, the 'Solar' series and 'Red Seven Star' are particularly outstanding.

Geranium For many people, red is the colour associated with geraniums but the options are gradually widening to include many shades of pink and even orange. There are also some novel bi-coloured varieties, like 'Hollywood Star' shown here.

Geranium (*Pelargonium*)   HHP

The last decade has seen a revolution in geraniums: whereas earlier plants were always raised as cuttings from well-known named varieties, almost all the present bedding types are grown from seed. Geraniums are prominent in public displays but their high cost does inhibit large-scale use in private gardens. The seed, which is expensive, must be sown in January if flowering is to commence by early June. Germination is no problem and occurs very quickly but the young plants need four months with the maximum light, and temperatures that do not fall below 10°C (50°F).

Varieties such as 'Century', 'Gala' and 'Diamond' have become the mainstream of geranium bedding but in the last few years there has been a significant breakthrough with 'Multibloom' and 'Sensation'. These varieties have many more flower heads than earlier hybrids and it is not unusual to have ten or even fifteen open at one time. The heads are not as large as previous varieties but can be used as a source of massed colour and there is the further bonus that both new hybrids come into flower about a fortnight earlier than the others. The leaf zoning is an attractive feature of most geraniums and although they prosper in dry weather, they give very acceptable results in damp summers.

'Jolly Joker' is a unique combination of pansy colours.

Pansy HP

Traditionalists may be reluctant to consider the pansy anything other than a spring subject, but plant breeders have produced new varieties to extend the season into the summer. The American 'Majestic Giants' and the Japanese 'Imperials' offer an unrivalled range of colour and the individual blooms have a spectacular beauty. Some like 'Imperial Antique Shades' and 'Love Duet' are unusual combinations of pastel shades, while 'Jolly Joker', 'Padparadja' and 'Rippling Waters' are strongly coloured.

Pansies excel in moist conditions and casualties will occur in long dry spells, but the seed germinates freely in a cool regime and the plants do not need coddling. The pansy is classified as a hardy perennial and therefore should appear year after year but most modern varieties are not reliable through winter and new plants must be grown regularly, either from seed or cuttings.

Petunia HHA

Like geraniums, petunias thrive in hot sunshine and are equally adept at resisting drought, but breeders have sought to improve their wet-weather image and they have succeeded. Many newer varieties like 'Dwarf Resisto' and 'Frenzy' have strengthened petals and they recover their poise after being battered by rainfall. Flowers are

Petunias are arguably the most dazzling of summer plants.

The 'Frenzy' series of petunias is outstanding.

produced as the stems extend and some plants may sprawl somewhat if some of the shoots are not pinched out to encourage basal growth.

Petunias are justifiably described as stunning bedding plants and some colours are so vivid that their effect can be overpowering. This is always a risk where mixed colours are sited together but there is ample choice of individual shades to blend with the rest of the display. Raising plants from seed is without complication and a mid-March sowing will ensure proper development for the normal bedding out time. It is the multiflora type of petunia that is most suitable for bedding purposes but the grandifloras, with huge flowers, are excellent for tubs and baskets where there is some shelter from wind and rain.

For many gardeners, the foregoing bedding plants represent everything that is required for a reliable summer show and nothing else is needed for prolonged colour. Some are better than others in sun or shade, wet or dry, but all perform well in less than ideal conditions. Many of these top performers can be retained from year to year because they are naturally perennial if protected

from frost. Specific favourites of geranium, busy lizzies and fibrous begonias, for instance, can be potted to provide out-of-season flowers in the home or greenhouse and cuttings can be taken in the spring.

The Best of the Rest

Many flowers may lack the exceptional features of the very best performers but some have few deficiencies and are able to bring new dimensions to summer bedding, such as subtlety, extra height, different flower forms, alternative hues and textural effects.

African Marigold   HHA

These are not subtle flowers! They produce bold colours and impressively large blooms in a restricted part of the spectrum. The plants vary from 30–90cm (1–3ft) in height but all have the huge flowers which many believe are out of scale. The flowers are also prone to rotting during prolonged wet weather but, like their French relatives, growth is rapid from seed. 'Perfection', the 'Incas' and the 'Jubilee' series are good varieties and are widely sold.

The brightness of 'Perfection' African marigolds is tempered by the muted shades of Rudbeckia 'Rustic Dwarfs'.

Ageratum (Floss Flower) HHA
Blue is the accepted colour but there are also whites and pinks and the latter are most appealing. The plants do look disagreeable when the blooms are dying, and deadheading is inconvenient, but the flowering period is quite long with adequate rainfall. 'Blue Champion' is the general favourite but the Dutch-bred 'Ocean' series is creditable in shades of blue and purple. Normal plants are 15–20cm (6–8in) tall but 'Blue Bouquet' and 'Wonder' are 30cm (12in) taller.

Alyssum (Alyssum) HA
In many gardens, the hardy nature of alyssum means that it appears each year from self-sown seedlings and it can reach weed proportions. Nonetheless, it is an old favourite edging plant and is only seriously deficient in prolonged dry spells. 'Snow Crystals', with larger than normal flowers, is the best white variety and 'Pastel Carpet' is an excellent mixture of white, pink and purple: 'Oriental Night' is a deep purple.

Antirrhinum (Snapdragon) HA
A much-loved plant of the last century and still fairly well received in recent times. The 'Coronettes' are 60cm (2ft) high with majestic flower spikes, but the shorter strains like 'Floral Carpet' and 'Cheerio' are increasingly favoured; 'Magic Carpet' is a dwarf at 15cm (6in). Plants grow slowly and must be sown early in the year but they are active members of the display for only about six weeks. If the seed pods are removed promptly, there will often be a further period of flowering.

Aster (*Callestephus*) HHA
There is great variation in flower form, and plant size ranges from 23–90cm (9–36in). Most catalogues list more than a dozen varieties. Asters begin flowering in mid-summer from a March sowing but the show continues until at least late September. Plants are susceptible to a fungus complaint

Asters start flowering late but the flowers are impressive.

called wilt and should not occupy the same part of the garden in successive years otherwise the infection can persist. 'Duchess' is a lovely taller variety and 'Pinocchio' is a good shorter one.

Carnation (*Dianthus*) HHA
Perennial carnations were regular residents of the old cottage gardens but their untidy habit has brought disfavour. New varieties, grown from seed, like 'Liliput' and 'Knight' have overcome this deficiency and are short and sturdy although not as fragrant as the old forms. Some seed-raised plants may survive through the winter but it is better to grow new

plants each year and plant them in garden soil where some lime is present.

Dahlia (*Dahlia*) HHP

These dazzling flowers are not to everyone's taste and are often accused of looking too perfect! Enthusiasts select from hundreds of named varieties but there are also numerous seed strains which enable a mass effect at very low cost. These are much shorter than their pedigree counterparts and do not need staking. A moist soil in full sun and regular feeding will ensure a succession of bloom until the first frost. Seed is large and germinates quickly and should be sown in April. Choice plants can be saved by

Named varieties of dahlia are spectacular as displayed in Southport's promenade gardens.

There are dozens of different dahlias to grow from seed, of which 'Collarette Dandy' is highly distinctive.

digging up the tubers and storing them away from frost during winter; these will provide cuttings in the spring.

Gazania (Treasure Flower) HHA

The spectacular colouring of gazanias has aroused increasing interest in recent years despite some drawbacks in cultivation. Plants are unhappy in heavy soil and the flowers close in late afternoon and do not open at all during dismal weather. Gazanias are surprisingly tough and are among the last flowers to be affected by autumn frosts; some plants will survive the winter in mild regions. Seed and plants are fairly expensive but only a few groups are needed in a mixed display.

Lobelia   HHA

This is another popular edging subject that has a long flowering period in good soil which does not dry out, and there are many varieties which have stood the test of time. 'Cambridge Blue' and 'Mrs Clibrans' are examples; 'Crystal Palace' is very eye-catching with its bronze foliage. The seed is tiny and difficult to sow evenly but the seedlings are not fussy and despite their slow growth, they are most reliable.

Many lobelia varieties have existed for generations, like the dark-leaved 'Crystal Palace'.

The modern nicotiana is not notably fragrant and the colours are not strong, but flowers appear throughout the summer.

Nicotiana (Tobacco Plant)   HHA

The forerunner of today's nicotiana was quite tall and had unremarkable flowers which closed during the day but had a wonderful scent in the evening and night. Plant breeders have produced the 'Nikki' and 'Domino' strains which are only 30cm (12in) tall and flower incessantly from early summer until the frosts arrive. Unfortunately, the scent is now hardly noticeable but flowers are open in daytime. Plants are easily obtained and home growers will have no trouble raising plants from seed.

Penstemon (Beard Tongue)   HHP

This is a splendid subject which has now gained the attention of the plant breeders and is not well known by the gardening public. The flowers are reminiscent of fox gloves except that the florets are arranged

Penstemon Strangely absent from most gardens, penstemons are beautiful flowers, reminiscent of small foxgloves. The plants are actually perennial but they are not reliably winter hardy. Grown as annuals and sown in the spring, their cultivation is simple.

Zinnia Good summers are a prerequisite for zinnias to perform at their very best but in a light soil that will not remain wet for prolonged periods, the results are usually good. Seed germinates readily and the plants grow fast from a late spring sowing.

around the stem instead of just on one side and the colours are limited to the pink, red and purple range. Plant height, depending on variety, is between 45 and 60cm (18 and 24in) and typified by the recognized leading strain called 'Skyline'.

Pinks (*Dianthus*) HHA, HP

The *dianthus* genus includes carnations but those that are commonly called pinks are mostly single-flowered, upright in habit and self-supporting. The 'Telstar' and 'Magic Charms' are no more than 23cm (9in) high and easily grown although, like carnations, they prefer well-drained soil which contains some lime.

Portulaca (Sun Plant) HHA

Vividly coloured flowers that look like mini-ature shrub roses are borne on dwarf plants with succulent foliage. A dry or very well-drained soil is helpful and, as the common name suggest, a sunny position is indispensable for a succession of summer blooms. 'Calypso', 'Sundance' and 'Cloudbeater' are well-proven strains and will be found in many catalogues.

Rudbeckia (Cone Flower) HHA

Large, daisy flowers with contrasting cone centres characterize these plants, which grow from 30–60cm (1–2ft) tall. 'Goldilocks' is the shortest; 'Marmalade' and 'Rustic Dwarf' are the taller end. Flowering is from early August until the autumn and the brown and golden shades make for a restful effect.

Sweet Pea (*Lathyrus*)   HA

Perhaps the most commonly purchased flower seed, the sweet pea is basically a climbing plant, although some short varieties do not need support. The taller kinds need a fence, wall, net or wigwam structure to display their great beauty, and they thrive in sunny places with ample supplies of water. Dozens of varieties in different colours are widely sold and names like 'Air Warden', 'Mrs R. Bolton' and 'Swan Lake' are legendary. The smaller strains, such as 'Knee Hi' and 'Snoopea' reach about 90cm (3ft), while 'Bijou' and 'Little Sweetheart' are about 30cm (12in). Smallest of all are only 15cm (6in) – 'Cupid' is one – and all these tiny plants can be used as conventional bedders.

Harlow Carr gardens in Yorkshire demonstrate the appeal of sweet peas.

Verbena *'Garden Party' and French marigold 'Aurora Fire'.*

Tithonia Mexican Sunflower   Tall plants are not very popular these days, but the Mexican Sunflower is a subject worth consideration because of its brilliant colouring. Sunshine and warmth are helpful for cultivation and seed should not be sown before late spring.

Verbena (*Verbena*)   HHA

Most verbenas are 20–25cm (8–10in) tall, showing pretty clusters of tiny florets in pink, red, lavender, blue, white and some bicolours. 'Garden Party' and 'Showtime' are well-tried varieties which grow reliably although germination of the seed will be poor in wet compost. The species *V. verbosa* has purple flowers and is 45cm (18in) tall.

Old Favourites

The summer bedding we have discussed so far are the most reliable and long-flowering subjects; some favourite flowers have been excluded simply because they do not satisfy the main criteria. However, many have considerable charm and are well worth attention.

Abutilon (Flowering Maple)   HHP
Althaea (Hollyhock)   HP, HA
Anchusa (Bugloss)   HA
Arctotis (African Daisy)   HHA
Brachycome (Swan River Daisy)   HHA
Calceolaria (Slipper Flower)   HHA
Calendula (Pot, or English, Marigold)   HA
Campanula (Canterbury Bell)   HB
Candytuft (*Iberis*)   HA
Chrysanthemum   HA
Clarkia   HA
Coreopsis (Tickseed)   HP
Cosmos (*Cosmea*)   HHA
Crepis (Hawksbeard)   HA
Delphinium (Larkspur)   HP, HA
Dimorphotheca (Star of the Veldt)   HHA
Eschscholzia (Californian Poppy)   HA
Gaillardia (Blanket Flower)   HHA, HP
Godetia   HA
Heliotrope (Cherry Pie)   HHA
Gypsophila (Baby's Breath)   HA
Lavatera (Mallow)   HA
Limnanthes (Poached, or Fried, Egg Plant)   HA
Lupin (*Lupinus*)   HP, HA
Matricaria (Feverfew)   HHA
Mesembryanthemum (Livingstone Daisy)   HHA
Mimulus (Monkey Flower)   HHA
Nasturtium (Tropaeolum)   HA
Nemesia   HHA
Nemophila (Baby Blue Eyes)   HA
Nigella (Love-in-a-Mist)   HA
Phacelia (Californian Bluebell)   HA
Phlox   HA
Salpiglossis (Painted Tongue)   HHA
Scabious (Cushion Flower)   HA
Schizanthus (Poor Man's Orchid or Butterfly Flower)   HHA
Tithonia (Mexican Sunflower)   HHA
Ursinia   HHA
Venidium (Monarch of the Veldt)   HHA
Zinnia (Youth and Old Age)   HHA

Chrysanthemum.

Cosmos.

Delphinium.

Nasturtium.

9 • SUMMER BEDDING: FEATURE PLANTS

Bedding displays are usually improved by the addition of the so-called dot plants to give some variety of height and texture. Foliage subjects are often used for the purpose, but there are also a number of flowers which will enhance the arrangement when suitably placed. Parks and public gardens often use tender perennials, but annuals can fill the role.

Abutilon (Flowering Maple)   HHS
Many of these handsome plants are ideal as contrasting features, but perhaps the most appealing is *A. striatum* 'Thompsonii', which has very distinctive, variegated leaves and grows to some 120 or 150cm (4 or 5ft). It is not available from seed; it must be raised from cuttings and overwintered in frost-free conditions.

Althaea Hollyhock   Modern hollyhocks have magnificently formed flowers, and some varieties are only 75cm (30in) tall, needing minimal support. A fungus disorder called rust afflicted the old perennial plants but this is unlikely to affect those grown as annuals.

Amaranthus (Love-Lies-Bleeding)   HHA
The unusual hanging tassels of blooms, in red, purple or green, are not to everyone's taste, but it is a useful feature plant, growing between 30 and 90cm (1 and 3ft).

Atriplex (Red Orache)   HA
The variety *A. purpurea* is especially useful as a quick-growing plant. It has dark-purple leaves and reaches about 120cm (4ft). Another is *A. hortensis cupreata*, whose foliage is deep red.

Brassica (Ornamental Cabbage)   HA
It may seem a bizarre choice for bedding but there are some highly coloured cabbages which might be considered for use amongst conventional bedding. It might stretch the gardener's imagination but there is an undoubted trend towards these technicolour culinaries, especially during winter when tubs and beds are otherwise bare.

Canna (Indian Shot)   HHP
A great favourite of parks' bedding designers, *Canna* is commonly seen with its tropical foliage and brilliant flowers. Those with bronze leaves are most favoured and prepackaged roots are available from garden centres, although many seed companies offer seed that will flower in the first summer from an early spring sowing. Blooms are typically red, but yellow, pink and cream are also available. The roots, like dahlia tubers, must be stored frost-free in winter.

Celosia (Prince of Wales Feathers)   HHA
These can be used as a main component of bedding schemes, particularly in a protected position. There are two basic sizes: those with plumes that reach 60cm (2ft) or so, and others which are half the size. Some thought should be given to co-ordinating the colour theme because some celosias have vivid colours and could look garish if they clash with the dominant hues.

Centaurea (Cornflower)   HHP
Many cornflowers are annual plants grown for their flowers but *C. candidissima* also displays charming silvery foliage which blends well with mixed colours. It makes an attractive feature plant that grows to 45cm (18in) tall.

Cerastium (Snow in Summer)   HP
Herbaceous borders often contain this plant for its white flowers, which appear in late spring. But since its foliage is also almost white, it is an effective foil for other flowers. The only drawback is its ability to spread rather quickly.

Cineraria maritima   HHP
Sometimes listed as *Senecio*, it is the most popular of the silver-leaf plants because it can be grown as an annual from seed without difficulty and can be planted out within a couple of months. The variety 'Silver Dust' is only 23 or 25cm (9 or 10in) high and can be incorporated into every conceivable bedding scheme. 'Cirrhus' is twice the height and has rounded leaves, but both varieties are quite hardy and frequently survive the winter, to grow much taller in subsequent years.

Coleus (Flame Nettle)   HHP
Another foliage plant that is commonly grown from seed but usually used as a pot plant for sunny windowsills. Many varieties are available. The colours are spectacular and they will normally succeed in the open garden, either in groups or as dot plants.

Cordyline
This is another tropical-looking subject that features in public displays in the midst of lower-growing flowers. *C. australis* and *C. indivisa* are the usual species, neither of which will survive anything but the mildest winter. Seed is occasionally offered but there is a lengthy germination period and growth is not rapid.

Eucalyptus (Gum Tree)   HHT
For foliar effect, the most common species is *E. globulus*, (the blue gum), whose lovely juvenile leaves are often used to accompany flower arrangements. Other species are also decorative while young but do not be tempted to leave these trees in the

Colour without flowers: Coleus *will succeed outdoors.*

garden for too long because many are surprisingly hardy and have the potential to reach over 18m (60ft) in a short time.

Euphorbia (Spurge)   HHA, HP
Spurges are highly rewarding for gardeners whose interests go beyond brightly coloured flowers because many have magnificently ornate foliage and can be grown very successfully from seed. One annual, 'Summer Icicle', has particularly striking white and green leaves.

Fuchsia HHP

Everyone knows and loves the fuchsia. Some are hardy in the garden, but few are cultivated as bedding subjects. They are ideal for raised beds where the flowers can be shown to advantage, but perhaps the best use is as standards which can be trained as fuchsia 'trees'. A stem of 90–120cm (3–4ft) can be grown over a two-year period and, if supported, can carry

Most fuchsias are entirely happy in the open garden.

hundreds of flowers almost at eye level. The stems are not immune to frost and they must be protected from winter temperatures.

Helichrysum petiolanum HHP

Without knowing its name, many home gardeners use these foliage plants in tubs and hanging baskets but very few utilize their attributes in the open garden. Three or four different varieties are widely offered at garden centres and they are entirely reliable as summer plants. The odd plant may survive the winter but not dependably.

Herbs HA, HP

Herbs are generally thought of as plants that fulfil a practical purpose, but a great number of them are highly decorative and they make an aesthetically pleasing contribution to the garden. Borage, fennel, sage and the dark-leaved basils are remarkable plants and thyme, rosemary and chamomile are long-standing occupants of beds and borders. Parsley deserves special mention since its tightly clustered, rich green foliage complements flowering subjects of all kinds.

Grasses HHA, HA, HP

Numerous ornamental grasses are available for adding interest, especially to areas of compact flowering plants, with a very different habit of growth. The soft, furry head of Hare's Tail and the pendulous pods of 'Briza' are appealing at low levels, while the silvery plumes of *Hordeum* and white or purple feathers of *Pennisetum* are more elevated. Some seed catalogues offer an intriguing selection.

Hypoestes (Polka Dot Plant) HHA

An irrepressible foliage pot plant, which is very much at home in the garden and adds considerable interest with compact neatness. Seed sown in the spring will produce plants for bedding out in summer, and a few different varieties are available.

Kochia (Burning Bush) HHA

The mature plants look like small conifers with a broad conical shape and superb, soft foliage which becomes richly tinted in the autumn. A temporary hedge of burning bush makes a beautiful boundary for bedding plants and will normally reach about 90cm (3ft).

Molucella (Bells of Ireland) HHA

Wherever it may be felt that strong colours need some relief, *molucella* is an ideal subject to convey a muted diversion. Its green, bell-shaped calyces are quietly distinctive and have a relaxing influence on the display.

Plectranthus coloides marginatus (Variegated Swedish Ivy)   HHP

The terrifying botanical name and misleading common name may be a deterrent but this is a most valuable foliage plant for baskets, tubs and beds and the bright variegation lends a cheerful aspect. It is sufficiently impressive to stand alone but makes a tasteful highlight amongst bedding, especially in sunny places. *Plectranthus* is not available from seed and is difficult to overwinter, even in a greenhouse, but the plants are commonly sold and cuttings root easily in spring.

Pyrethrum   HP, HHA

Daisy flowers are associated with this genus but one species, *P. aureum*, is invaluable for its conspicuous, green-yellow leaves. The variety 'Golden Moss', sometimes listed as *Parthenium*, grows 10–13cm (4–5in) high and allows intermingling with small flowers.

Ricinus (Castor Oil Plant)   HHA

Noted as a rugged houseplant, the bronze-leaved varieties of *Ricinus* give a tropical look to the garden. Tall varieties like 'Carmencita' are popular in parks but 'Impala' is more suited to small gardens. Attractive while young, it grows to 120cm (4ft) and the deep red colouring of the large, shapely leaves is most impressive.

Swiss Chard   HA

Many years ago, numerous members of the beet family were grown for decoration and a few examples remain in the vegetable sections of current catalogues. One, often called 'Ruby', has red stems and leaf-ribs, and a seed mixture called 'Swiss Rainbow' produces plants with white or red stems and rich green leaves. Growth habit is orderly

Venidium Monarch of the Veldt   The deficiencies of lax growth and untidy foliage are amply compensated for by the intricate beauty of the blooms, which can be 10cm (4in) across. The flowers deserve their common name: 'Orange Surprise', shown here, is a magnificent example.

and attains about 38cm (15in). Like the colourful cabbages, chard is also edible.

Zea (Sweet Corn)   HHA

Yet another vegetable that can be used for contrasting effect, but like some other feature plants it must be used in moderation otherwise it overpowers the display. The variety 'Quadricolour' has a red tinge on the green and white leaves and does not usually bear cobs, but with 'Strawberry Corn', the dark red cobs are the main attraction. Most sweet corn grows to about 120cm (4ft).

10 • DISEASE AND PEST PROBLEMS

Bedding plants are not especially prone to disease, but as with all plants, there is always the possibility that a problem may arise. Plants have their own immune systems and those that are grown well are especially able to resist attacks from pests and combat the affliction of disease. The majority of gardens will escape the plagues that are potentially threatening to the high concentration of similar plants that are found on commercial holdings and arable farms: the great diversity of subjects in gardens protects from widespread infestation by pests and inhibits the progress of disease organisms. If substantial damage appears to be likely it is essential to seek the advice of experienced gardeners, either from the local allotment society or the local authority. Here we shall consider those disorders that are most commonly found.

Limnanthes Poached Egg Plant   Greatly loved by insect life, this plant is despised by some gardeners because it succeeds year after year without attention and is often treated as a weed. Early summer would not be the same without its cheerful brightness.

Diseases

There are hundreds of fungal diseases that can affect plant life and, they are most prevalent when climatic conditions are conducive to their flourishing. However, with luck, only three may be encountered in a domestic garden.

Botrytis

In persistent humid conditions, the stems and leaves of bedding plants can be invaded by a grey, woolly mould which sometimes gains a hold in the flowers and spreads to other parts. It should not cause alarm because removing the affected parts from the plant is usually sufficient to limit the contamination. However, if it worsens and becomes evident on other plants, treatment with a fungicide is advised.

Damping Off

Seedlings that are overcrowded and grown in a very humid atmosphere are sometimes infected by fungus that strikes at the base of the stem and causes the plant to collapse. This nuisance is invariably traced to unsterilized soil and the danger is virtually eliminated by using new compost for sowing seeds and washing trays in a mild disinfectant before sowing. Where damage occurs, it can be arrested by watering with a solution of Cheshunt compound and where expensive seed is being sown it is a wise precaution to use this chemical from the beginning.

Mildew

Two types of mildew occur, often in totally different circumstances. Powdery mildew is encouraged by dry weather and is evidenced by a white deposit which spreads if corrective measures are not taken. Downy mildew is prevalent in damp, still conditions and the leaves show signs of yellowing caused by the fungal infection on the underside. In both cases, removal of the affected parts is the first step followed by a spray with a proprietary fungicide.

Pests

All disease, by definition, is unwelcome but many insects make a legitimate living from vegetation and in many instances they are quite benign. But some do cause real damage. The most difficult to detect and eradicate are those that live in the soil, such as wireworm, cutworm and the grubs of the vine weevil. If plants collapse or deteriorate rapidly without visible cause, it is sensible to apply a soil insecticide but the majority of attacks are above ground and the following list identifies the main culprits.

Aphids

These ever-present creatures are not always green; they come in various colours. A large colony may overwhelm growing shoots, but small groups are not to be feared. It should be remembered that aphids are an important food source for small birds and the larvae of many beneficial insects like ladybirds. If the aphid presence is very large, they are easily killed by insecticides but caring gardeners will want to confine themselves to using sprays that have minimal toxicity. Some are based on insecticidal soap, which is relatively harmless to other insects, but even a forceful jet of plain water or a heavy shower of rain will dislodge large numbers of aphids and keep them under control.

Caterpillars

A bad infestation can cause untold havoc, but most gardeners are mindful of the fact that caterpillars are part of the lifecycle of moths and butterflies. Wholesale destruction will limit the populations of these creatures without which our gardens would be sorely deficient. It is a question of scale and most gardeners will take the view of live and let live unless the well being of a particular plant is threatened.

Earwigs

Mass invasions are undocumented but these armour-plated insects can cause domestic damage to flowers, especially dahlias and chrysanthemums. Observations suggest that earwigs are the Jekyll and Hyde of the insect world: in early summer they prey on many garden pests, but later on in the year they turn their attention to flowers and nibble the petals. At this time they are susceptible to insecticide powders applied below the blooms or at the base of the stems.

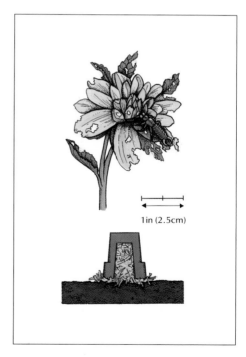

1in (2.5cm)

An inverted plant pot stuffed with straw is the traditional trap for earwigs, which cause considerable damage to the flowers of many plants – especially dahlias and chrysanthemums – in the late summer. Insecticide powders can also be used.

Capsid Bugs

Mostly, these sap-sucking enemies cause only slight damage to the leaves but in a bad season the foliage becomes distorted and developing flower buds can be casualties. Unfortunately, only the systemic insecticides are effective and spraying must start when the first signs are seen.

The characteristic tunnels of leaf-miner larvae.

Leaf-Miner

These are an irritant rather than a threat to the plant's health but the larvae can turn foliage into an unsightly mess. The fly, which looks like a housefly, lays eggs on the underside of leaves and, after hatching, the larvae burrow between the outer membranes causing the characteristic tunnels. Removing the ruined leaves and squashing the grubs is one option but it is difficult to prevent attacks without frequent use of systemic preparations.

Slugs

Unquestionably, the attentions of these soft-bodied monsters can devastate plants overnight and most gardeners put them at the top of the hit list. They are nocturnal and enjoy wet conditions, and few gardens are immune to their voracious appetites. A resident hedgehog is the most desirable, natural enemy of the slug because, although birds are enthusiastic predators, slugs are rarely active after dawn when birds are likely to be feeding.

Numerous imaginative ideas for slug control have been put forward, some have their roots firmly in folklore, others depend on the use of modern technology, but each has its limitations which means that slug pellets are really the only practicable protection. There is justifiable concern that this method can be dangerous for pets and other animals but the modern pellet has been designed to reduce these drawbacks. The most recent idea, which is currently undergoing research, is the use of a parasite whose common host is the garden slug. The parasite is purposely introduced to the garden where it attacks and eventually kills the slug population. Its use has two main advantages: it attacks slugs both above and below ground, ensuring that control is almost absolute, and it would appear to be harmless to other animals and insects. However, until this method is fully tested and available, pellets remain the most effective slug-killer.

Newly planted bedding is at greatest risk and it would be foolhardy to neglect the simple precaution of sprinkling pellets around the whole area. There are a number of different slugs that inhabit gardens but the only meaningful classification depends on the size of the body – and hence the size of the mouth. Some of the liquid slug treatments are useful for killing those that are

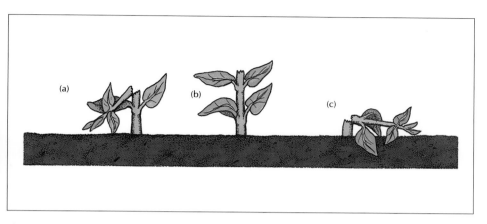

Slug damage to bedding plants is variable. If the stem is eaten part way up (a), the plant will often survive; if the tip only is destroyed (b), survival is almost certain, but where the stem is severed below the bottom leaves (c), death is likely.

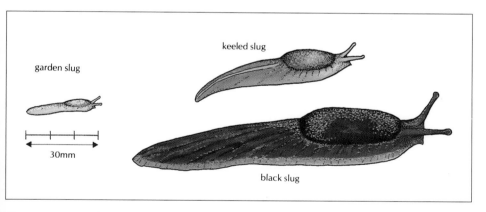

The most common slugs.

under the soil but subsequent rainfall does diminish their effect.

Pets

Dogs and cats are an integral part of many households but there is no doubt that they constitute a major threat to young bedding. Unfortunately, the many widely advertised deterrents are unlikely to prove satisfactory and, again, rainy weather reduces what effect they have. Perhaps the only solution is to demonstrate to your pets, kindly but firmly, that beds and borders are 'no-go' areas.

11 • THE LAST WORD IN BEDDING

Sales figures over recent years show that bedding plants are increasingly popular and also indicate that there is an increasing preference for buying plants as opposed to seed. Perhaps this is because many home owners are interested in enhancing the domestic environment but do not wish to devote time and attention to raising their own plants. The sales figures may also reveal that seed has an image problem with new generations of gardeners who believe that it presents complications and is inherently prone to failure. This is a pity because growing from seeds means that you have a vast choice of variety and type, and, I find as much fulfilment in the preparation of a beautiful display as I do in the realization. There is immense competition for our leisure time and it is hoped that everyone will be able to select those areas of gardening that appeal most and reject the remainder. Whether you pursue gardening for its ornamental results or as an enthralling hobby, or both, I hope that this book enables you to achieve more success and enjoyment. May your weeds wither and your flowers flourish!

A summer bed in the author's garden just after planting.

The same bed six weeks later.

GLOSSARY

Acid (soil)   Having a pH below 6.5.
Alkaline (soil)   Having a pH above 7.5.
Annual   Plant that matures and completes its life cycle within one year.
Axil   The angle formed by the stem and leaf stalk.
Axillary   A shoot arising from an axil.

Ball   The formation of roots in a container.
Bicolour   A flower in a combination of two distinct colours.
Biennial   A plant that takes two years to complete its lifecycle.
Bottom heat   Artificially produced heat applied to the base of a propagator.

Calcareous   Describes soil containing chalk or lime.
Cultivar   Garden variety of plant, or form found in the wild and maintained as a clone in cultivation.
Cutting   A portion of the living root, stem or leaf, taken from a plant and used for propagation.

Deadheading   Removal of dead flowers from a plant in order to encourage the growth of more flowers.
Dibber   A cylindrical tool, usually made of wood or plastic, used to make planting holes for seedlings.
Double   Describes a flower with multiple layers of petals.
Drill   A straight shallow furrow made in the soil, into which seeds are sown.

Entire   Smooth continuous edges to the leaf margin.
Eye   Undeveloped growth bud; also used to describe the centre of a flower.

Family   A botanical category of plants containing one or more genera with similar flower construction.
F₁ Hybrid   The first-generation plant produced from two distinct parent strains. It is usually vigorous.

Fertilizer   Chemical that provides plant food.
Floriferous   Free flowering.

Genus (plural, genera)   The next category down from family, containing one or more species.
Germination   The point at which a seed first begins growth.

Habit   Manner of growth.
Hybrid   A plant grown from seed resulting from a cross between two distinct species.

pH   A scale that measures acidity or alkalinity: a pH of between 6.5 and 7.5 is neutral; below 6.5 is acid; above 7.5 is alkaline.
Pinching   Removal of a growing tip to encourage a plant to produce side-shoots, thus promoting bushy growth.
Prickout   To transplant seedlings.
Propagation   To raise a plant by sowing seed, or by taking a cutting from the parent plant.

Single   Describes a flower with a single layer of petals.
Species   The category of plant, within a genus, as found in the wild. Plants of a species are genetically similar and will breed true to type from seed.
Stopping   *See* pinching.

Tender   Susceptible to serious or fatal damage by low temperatures.

Variegated   Describes leaves that are made up of two colours, usually a combination of green with yellow, cream or white markings.
Variety   Strictly, this is a variation of a species that occurs in the wild, but the term is more often used to describe cultivars – in other words, named varieties.

Watering in   To apply water around newly planted roots.

INDEX